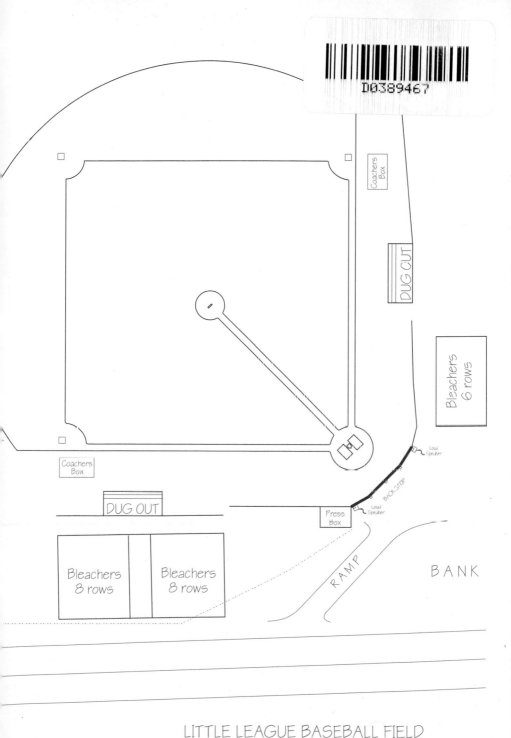

LITTLE LEAGUE BASEBALL FIELD
MAX M. BROWN MEMORIAL PARK   WILLIAMSPORT, PA.

10 - 25 - 1945

CARL E. STOTZ

A PRMISE KEPT

THE STORY OF THE FOUNDING
OF LITTLE LEAGUE BASEBALL

BY

CARL E. STOTZ

AS TOLD TO

KENNETII D. LOSS

EDITED BY

STEPHANIE R. ZEBROWSKI

ZEBROWSKI HISTORICAL SERVICES
PUBLISHING COMPANY
JERSEY SHORE, PA.
1992

Published by:
Zebrowski Historical Services Publishing Company
RR 1 Box 400, Jersey Shore, Pennsylvania 17740
1-800-753-3727.

First Edition.

Library of Congress Number: 92-062076
ISBN 1-880484-05-6

Edited by Stephanie R. Zebrowski
Designed by Mark Davis of Endless Productions,
Illustrated by C.A. Pijacki
Special Thanks to Gary W. Mowery

DEDICATION

With profound respect and appreciation, we
dedicate this book to the thousands of dedicated
volunteers who caught the vision of what might be
and worked as one to make the dream come true for
baseball-loving youngsters everywhere.

Editor's Preface

When Carl Stotz took a small group of kids out to a seldom used ball field one warm summer evening in 1938, carefully measuring off the distance between each base, he was considering the boys. If the field and equipment were designed just for them, wouldn't it be more fun? He had wished for that, himself.

Carl couldn't have envisioned modern Little League, as we know it. It has become the most commonly known children's athletic program in the world. There are Little Leagues on every continent, in 63 countries involving 180,000 teams. More specifically, there are 2.6 million children and 750,000 volunteers involved in Little League today.

The kids are everything in Little League now, just as they were when Carl Stotz ran the program. Little League Baseball, Inc., has taken Carl's concern into other areas that affect children's lives. They have developed a drug and alcohol prevention program and a movie featuring major-league stars, for distribution to all leagues. They are currently piloting an "anti-spitting tobacco" program in the seven states where use of smokeless tobacco is most prevalent. Developed in conjunction with Dr. Louis Sullivan, Secretary of Health and Human Services, it will eventually go out to all leagues.

Little League Baseball, Inc., also has a new inner-city program. They have developed an adult-volunteer education program stressing that the game is for the kids; the adults are there as supervisors and role models. They publish literature dealing with emotional stability to help insure that Little League will be a healthful experience. Emergency field management training has been incorporated into the program along with umpire training programs and a summer camp for Little Leaguers and umpires.

The Challenger Division is providing some unexpected results, just as Carl experienced during his years with Little League. The Challenger Division is comprised of youngsters who are mentally or physically handicapped. The Division includes volunteer "buddies" of Little League age, to push a wheel chair to base, or whatever. Since buddies are not related to the kids they're helping, they develop an awareness and sensitivity to the needs of others outside the program. It is a reflection of attitudes that develop when kids learn the rewards of volunteering. Already, the program has over 1,000 teams involving 15,000 players.

According to Carl, volunteers have always been the backbone of Little League. That is still true. Just as the kids in Little League are everything, so are the volunteers. Each year, Volunteer of the Year awards are given out in every region. Little League Baseball, Inc., also honors other outstanding volunteers with awards such as the *William A. Shea Distinguished Little League Graduate Award,* which goes to former Little leaguers involved in the majors. In 1992, the award went to Steve Palermo, who had been shot in the back when he tried to aid strangers. Told he would never walk again, he appeared on crutches to accept his award. When he was introduced as a former umpire, he replied, "That's not true, I will return." His attitude, courage, character, and loyalty exemplify Little League as Carl envisioned it.

Carl always held the best interest of the boys paramount. What is best for them is best for Little League. Usually that meant building self-esteem, teaching them to be proud of their efforts to play well so that trying a little harder the next time will come naturally. Carl would agree with the reasoning that led Little League Baseball, Inc., to go to a round-robin system during the World Series. Because some of the children travel half-way around the world to get to Williamsport, they are not over jet lag by game time. And, they are under pressure. This way, they can have a bad day and still come out on top.

Carl's other important ingredient, magic, is still part of the program, too. In 1992, as in the past, all player-participants were awarded identical medals. Usually, they are awarded during a private dinner. However, this year, they were awarded like Olympic medals, before cheering crowds.

Carl Stotz wanted to give children a little magic, a safe environment in which to play, and the desire to do well by oneself and others. He could not have known how large his dream would grow, but he did know that it could. He believed it would help children and it was the right thing for him to pursue. He used to laugh when remembering the time someone told him they knew he was dedicated when he was spotted at 5 a.m., working on Little League Field!

Everyone who got to know Carl well was affected by him. There was something special about him and the way he touched people that made him capable of organizing one of the largest volunteer programs in the world. I feel fortunate to have known him.

I am also pleased to have had the opportunity to work with Ken Loss. His wry sense of humor and professionalism made working with him a pleasure. His constant striving for perfection and accuracy and delight in his craft were a pleasure to behold.

Chapter 1

Somewhere deep inside, beyond my consciousness, the love of baseball lay waiting for an opportunity to get out. I was 28 and happily married, father of a two-year-old daughter, content with life just as it was.

I had lived and breathed baseball nearly a decade ago, when I seized every opportunity to play the game. I had even thought about a professional career, until I realized my size and limited natural ability would never allow it. And now, much as I loved the sport, I seldom attended professional games, though I suppose my limited income made that an easy decision. Even so, radio broadcasts were popular, but I seldom listened. I was busy with other things.

Being a little boy who never grew up, as some have since described me, I spent a lot of time playing with my sister's younger sons, Jimmy, who was six, and Harold "Major" Gehron, eight. We were together all the time. Since I was chief clerk for the Pure Oil Company in Williamsport, Pennsylvania — there weren't any other clerks, but that was my title — one of my job responsibilities was to deposit the previous day's receipts at the bank downtown. I used to stop at my sister's house at noon and pick up the boys, who were always raring and ready to go. Sometimes their older brother, Carl, would join us on our outings, but my constant companions were Jimmy and Major.

Though baseball, to the best of my knowledge, was behind me, it was not so for the boys, for despite their ages, they were already avid fans. Occasionally, they were able to attend Class A games at Bowman Field when the Williamsport Grays were in town. But, when they couldn't, they listened to sportscaster Sol Wolf's colorful play-by-play coverage over radio-station WRAK. The excitement of Eastern League baseball had captivated them. Perhaps inspired by their older brother, they mimicked the colorful language Sol Wolf used in his daily broadcasts. In their little-boy way they tried to duplicate the spectacular fielding feats he so often described in terms that, to them, quickly became synonymous with baseball.

Major would throw a "line drive" across the back-yard just high enough that Jimmy would have to run and stretch as far as he could to catch it. All the while, Major would keep up a running commentary a la Sol Wolf.

"And there goes a line drive DEEP into center field. Jimmy Gehron is going back, back. Is it out of here? No! Gehron leaps high against the boards and makes a be-yew-tu-ful backhand snag of the ball. I'm telling you, ladies and gentlemen, he robbed 'em that time. Listen to that applause!"

When Jimmy threw the ball back, he would provide the Sol Wolf commentary as Major made the play.

Dramatic as they made the game seem, they were playing the game mostly in their imaginations ... two little boys imagining the other players, managers, coaches, umpires, the excitement of the crowd, and the radio broadcaster. Unfortunately, the backyard was too confining to risk batting. Even a poorly *thrown* ball could have gotten one into trouble with the neighbors.

On what was, in retrospect, a very special summer day in 1938, those two little boys rekindled my long-dormant enthusiasm for baseball, whipping it into the bright flame of Little League baseball for small boys.

Jimmy and Major showed up at my house, running as usual. They were breathless, but not speechless. As they arrived, each thumping his fist into his glove, one said, "Uncle Tuck, let's play catch."

Rarely needing a second invitation from those two, I moved quickly into action with them in my yard. The game was as much fantasy as reality to them as they returned throws with their best imitations of the Eastern Leaguers.

On one throw, Major heaved the ball out of Jimmy's reach and I had to move quickly to the neighbors' side of the yard. We shared a double yard with a family named Flickenger at that time. As I stretched to catch the ball, I stepped into the cut off stems of a lilac bush that were projecting several inches above the ground. A sharp stub tore through my sock and scraped my ankle. It did no serious damage, but the immediate pain was intense, so I hobbled to the Flickenger's back-porch steps and sat down until the pain eased. The boys came running and sat on the steps beside me. As soon as they were sure I wasn't seriously hurt, they resumed their baseball chatter.

The aftermath of my accident somehow turned into a magic moment. As I sat there rubbing my ankle, listening to those two little boys, I had what you might call a flashback, when everything seems to be right there in front of you. That's what I saw as I sat on those back steps. I was playing right field again, waiting for the other team's last batter to strike out so I could have my turn at bat. Impatiently wishing they would speed things up a bit, I had thought to myself, "When I grow up, I'm gonna have a baseball team for boys, complete with uniforms and equipment. They'll play on a real field like the big guys, with cheering crowds at every game."

"How would you like to play on a regular team, with uniforms and a new ball for every game and bats you can really swing?" I asked Jimmy and Major.

Their beaming faces expressed their unspoken enthusiasm for the idea. But, they immediately became very practical about it.

"Uncle Tuck, who will we play?"

It was a good question. I remembered, but didn't tell them about a game we'd had with the Scott Street Sluggers when I was a kid. When the Sluggers came down to our field to play, most of the boys had on bib overalls like the kind farmers wore. One boy was even barefoot. It wouldn't be any fun for a team of uniformed players to play with boys who didn't have uniforms, so I just said, "You won't have any trouble getting another team from another neighborhood."

"Do you think people will come to watch us play?"

"I don't know," I said, "but there's a good chance some will. I'm sure your parents will come. And the neighbors, when they see your uniforms, will come."

"Do you think a band will ever come?"

They were probably thinking of the Grays' season opener at Bowman Field. A band played before the game and between innings. I certainly couldn't promise a band and an audience at their games, but I enjoyed dreaming of the possibility as much as they did. Years later, when Jimmy and I were recalling those moments, I still wondered where they got the idea for a band. Looking over old photographs, it came to me. Tree-climbing being a natural pastime of little boys, they must have climbed the tree in their front yard to look over their territory. They must have been able to see all the way to the trolley junction and beyond. That had been a parade route on occasion. I could picture those two little boys sitting up there in that tree, thrilled to hear the marching band playing their way down the street and out of sight. Their imaginations had given flight to their ideas. Funny though it might seem, at the time it was just as serious to me as it was to them.

Several days later, I asked Major and Jimmy to speak to some of their friends about becoming part of a team. They kept me posted as they recruited them, and I set a time for our first training session.

I picked up the boys in my car and we drove out to what in now the "Carl E. Stotz Field." We walked out to a spot, now mid-left field, where the grass had been worn, showing spots where the batter and pitcher stood when picnickers played there. I brought along a bat and a fairly decent ball and several newspapers to fold into bases. Some of the boys had their own gloves and willingly shared with those who did not.

After I placed the papers around the field to represent home plate and each base, I positioned the boys around the infield while I served as pitcher. From time to time, I changed the distance between the bases. I was trying to find out what distance would enable the boys to throw a runner out from third base or shortstop while still giving the batter a fair chance to beat it out, depending on where he hit the ball.

Night after night I squeezed the boys into my black 1934 Plymouth two-door sedan — it was quite a crowd — and took them to practice in the park. Each evening, I continued experimenting with the distance between bases. When I finally had what I thought was the ideal distance, I stepped it off and used a yardstick at home to measure my strides. The distance was so close to sixty feet that I set that as the distance we would use thereafter.

I was also concerned about the distance between home plate and the pitching rubber, which we didn't have yet. Home plate was also missing at this point. I was dealing with a matter of a few feet and inches, for I knew the distance had to be roughly proportionate to the distance between the bases as it is on an adult-sized diamond, and within a boy's ability to throw accurately.

Meanwhile, the boys were having the time of their lives. They were certainly as enthusiastic about their play as I was about the idea of planning and organizing a league for them.

Organized baseball for small boys might easily have died at birth, for just as I was getting the pilot going, I lost my job. Fortunately, summer was almost gone. That gave me breathing room to find a job that would enable me to work with Jimmy, Major, and their friends again when the next baseball season rolled around.

Chapter 2

The year 1938 had begun as one of promise for the Stotz family. Grayce and I had a 16-month-old daughter, Monya Lee, and I had a new job as head clerk for Pure Oil Company. Our finances were in order. We were optimistic about the future. Actually, things were better than I realized.

Early in the spring, I had a job offer from a plumbing-supply house to work on commission as a salesman. I declined the offer, unwilling to depend on my sales ability for a living. I preferred a fixed-pay job with regular hours, so I continued to work at Pure Oil.

That summer, the local soft-drink bottler, Z.H. "Dick" Confair, stopped in to buy lubricating oil for the machinery in his plant. I had no idea, while I stood there chatting with him, about the type of machinery he had, nor that this chance meeting would have as much future significance for me as my playing ball with Major and Jimmy would prove to have.

I felt so secure then that I never considered that my job could be in jeopardy. But, progress made its way to Williamsport in the form of a new pipeline across the mountains. Pure's gasoline supply was brought into the city by railroad tank car. With pipeline deliveries coming to the competition at a cheaper rate, Pure Oil found itself with no choice but to discontinue its operation in Williamsport. To most people who read about it in the newspapers, Pure Oil's closing was just one of those things; Pure Oil Company had become a victim of progress. Company employees were victims, too.

For the second time in three years, I was a draftee in the vast Depression army of the unemployed. The economy was still in a tailspin and would remain in a tailspin until World War II turned it around. Since Grayce had always worked and we had a pretty conservative lifestyle, we were keeping our heads above water and putting money in the bank. Until the second week in September, we survived on Grayce's income and my $12.10 unemployment check every two weeks. When, at last, I spotted a nearby venetian-blind manufacturer's "Help Wanted" ad in a local paper, I soon found myself hired for the night shift.

One night was enough. I had never done factory work and had no idea what it would be like. Worse, I was assigned to the department that dip-painted the blinds in a large vat which gave off such an offensive odor that it penetrated every pore of my body and clung to my clothes long after I left the plant. The stench was still with me when I got home, and it stuck around even after we opened the windows! I didn't resist when Grayce suggested I look for other work.

Once again the unexpected occurred and I found myself able to produce an income, this time from our vacant lot. I had been preparing the lot for the day when Grayce and I would finally build our own home. I had landscaped the prospective yard and now had some sale-able items and a pretty fair degree of expertise in handling them.

As it happened, I was out job hunting when I passed the Harrington Ice Cream Plant and noticed they had an addition under construction. I went home and drew up a landscaping plan for it, using all the nursery stock from my own propagation beds. I put together a detailed brochure, using colorful cutouts from nursery catalogs along with scale drawings, and presented it to the company manager. He was pleased enough to hire me for the job. I suspect, though, that the price was a factor, since I did the entire job for $40. Ultimately, it wasn't the money that would be most valuable to me, it was the self-confidence I gained from the experience.

I continued to try to find work. In early October, I answered an ad for a local hardware and lumber company. They were looking for someone to replace an employee who had come into a little money and decided to retire. The interview went well, and I was being considered for the job. But, when I didn't hear from them as soon as I had expected, I returned to find that the employee had changed his mind about retiring.

Disappointing as that was, I decided I would like to work for a lumber company. I had long been interested in home-building. I had even designed a compact little house comparable to a modern mobile home. I called it the Tuckaway, combining my nickname with the fact that it was small and used space efficiently, providing all necessities and a comfortable living room as well.

I now approached Richard H. Lundy, head of Lundy Construction Company, even though he hadn't advertised for help. He wasted no time telling me there were "no openings at present." He did take a look at my drawings, though, and asked me a few questions, so I left feeling encouraged.

My next call was on my former customer, Dick Confair. He, too, told me he'd hire me if he could, but there were no openings. Except for that one-night stand as a factory worker and my landscaping venture, I had been unemployed for two months.

Then N.R. Richards, my boss at Pure Oil, called to tell me he had acquired an interest in Thomas Fuel and Oil of Bellefonte and had a job for me if I wanted it. That's how I became a retail-service-station operator, company record keeper of wholesale accounts, and a five-day-a-week resident of Bellefonte.

When I went to my car after the first night, it was covered with a fine layer of lime dust from the nearby stone quarry and lime-manufacturing plant. That, the cost of living away from home, the dead-end nature of the job, and my desire to stay in Williamsport with my family convinced me the job wasn't for me. At the end of the week, I thanked Mr. Richards for his offer and returned to Williamsport with the $12 I had earned.

Back home again, I called at Richard Lundy's office. He was very encouraging, saying something might open up soon for me. It did. I went to work November 1, 1938.

My drawings and persistence had paid off, for my first assignment was to make scale drawings of the interiors of a row of old brick houses being remodeled for Lycoming College. Although the temperature in the houses was near freezing and my only tool was a six-foot folding ruler, I mapped out the debris-laden rooms, overjoyed at being involved in the home-construction industry.

Within four weeks, though, I was once again among the unemployed. Lundy's had won the contract to build Clarke Chapel for the college and needed someone with more knowledge and experience. Waiting until the week after Christmas to break the news to me, Mr. Lundy suggested I speak to his brother, Jack, about a possible opening at Lundy Lumber Company. Dick Lundy kept me on his payroll for another two weeks until I began working for Lundy Lumber.

It seemed that nothing could top 1938 for exciting living, but that was hindsight, not foresight. Because of my commitment to Jimmy and Major, each year for the next decade and a half would provide a continuing series of challenges, opportunities, struggles, emotional highs and lows, and the certainty that I was doing something worthwhile.

I was not aware of it at the time, but the challenge of finding a job had provided valuable training in a discipline that would soon be severely tested as I sought sponsors for small boys' baseball teams. It was simply the ability to keep knocking on doors until someone responded favorably. I was prepared for the great adventure that was to follow.

When I began work for Lundy Lumber in mid-January, 1939, the training process continued. Lundy's had bought out a lumber company in nearby Hughesville and another one in Muncy. They now had a big backlog of unpaid bills. I was to be the bill collector. I had to learn to combine tact with boldness and schedule calls at the most opportune time. My calls always had a sharply defined purpose!

I also filled in at the sales counter and machine-posted the customers' ledger accounts for the bookkeeper. I worked at the sales counter at the beginning and close of the day when the carpenters usually came in to buy supplies. Within limits, I could post accounts whenever I found time, since I worked alone. In extremely busy periods during the summer, I sometimes did it at night. Then, when the Grays were playing at home, I could hear the fans cheering at Bowman Field.

Chapter 3

During those difficult months of job-hunting and learning new employment roles, I did little or nothing outwardly to keep the promise I had made to my nephews, though I was constantly thinking of possible ways to form teams for a league.

I knew I had to change playing rules to conform to the age and size of the boys. Heretofore, small boys had been trying to play on corner lots or diamonds designed for men, or on corner lots with rules that changed from game to game. I was groping to find a uniformity that all who became involved in my baseball league would willingly abide by because it was right for the kids.

When I'd begun to play sandlot ball 20 years earlier, when I was nine, nothing was geared to children. We'd step up to the plate with a bat that was both too heavy and too long. Choking up on the bat merely changed the problem. The handle would then bang us in the stomach when we lunged at the ball. We didn't have the strength or leverage for a smooth, controlled swing.

The batter wasn't the only one with problems. The pitcher was too far away to throw hard enough to be effective, so he simply aimed the ball over the plate. The catcher, without a mask, chest protector, or shin guards, stooped over near the backstop, when there was one. The ball usually came to him on a bounce, making him more of a retriever than a catcher.

Fielders were at a disadvantage, too. Only the batter had any kind of advantage. When he hit the ball solidly, he usually made it safely to first base. From there, he could advance almost at will. Most of the time when he attempted to steal, the throw was late and off target or overthrown, allowing the runner to take an extra base. Once on third, he stood a very good chance of scoring on a passed ball. As a result, scores were usually high for both teams. An adult-sized diamond and adult rules made sound defense impossible for young boys.

Even the gloves that some of the boys had were poorly designed for catching. They were flat and ill formed for little hands since they were made primarily to protect. One had to move the bare hand atop the ball with perfect timing the moment it arrived to keep it in the glove. Designed for adults, the fingers were so long and flat that children couldn't keep them from flexing back when the ball missed the center of the glove. A cheap, old glove was often referred to disdainfully as a "dishrag." Even the ball was a problem in my sandlot days. Often we'd start out with some one's castoff, the leather cover missing or about ready to fall off. We would use the same ball over and over again until it literally fell apart. Once in a while someone would come up with a brand-new ball. We would bat it around until the threads wore out and the leather cover fell off. Then, we'd wrap it with tire tape, time and time again, until there was nothing left to salvage.

As winter wore on, I continued to look back at baseball the way I had played it as a boy. I became more determined than ever to make the changes that would transform the game from a sandlot "game of the imagination" into a "real game."

I concluded, right away, that the rule allowing the batter to try to reach first base on a dropped third strike had to eliminated. It also seemed necessary to create a rule to prevent runners from taking a lead off base before the ball passed home plate. I believed those changes were the solution to the most apparent problems. Besides, I thought that if the boys were forced to earn their runs, they would enjoy the game more.

I had already decided during our training sessions at Memorial Park the summer before to shorten the distance between the bases from 90 feet to 60. I had also decided that the number of innings should be reduced from nine to six. These were little boys I was planning for, after all.

I had also decided that it would be best to provide a new, good-quality, standard adult-sized ball for each game. I didn't want anything to do with the cheap, easy-to-get, poor-quality youth-sized balls that became lopsided after a little use. At the time, the standard adult-sized balls were an important factor because the boys always seemed to be able to get hold of used ones for personal practice. If I were to require special-size balls in the organized league I envisioned, parents would have to buy them for their boys to practice with away from the playing field. Remember, this was 1938 when I was making these decisions, and the Great Depression was still with many American families. I was afraid the expense would be too much for some families and might keep boys from becoming Little Leaguers.

Though I had given plenty of thought to the distance from the pitching rubber to home plate and the size of home plate, I had not decided exactly what they should be. Just before the first official Little League game, June 6, 1939, I finally resolved the problem. I set the pitching distance at 38 feet and the width of home plate at 14-$\frac{1}{8}$-inches.

By the time the season opened, Jimmy and Major were seven and nine years old. At the time, I thought the game should be for boys like my nephews and their friends. Experience quickly showed, however, that it would have to be geared to slightly older boys, as well. The following winter, the field managers I had recruited reviewed the age restrictions and decided it would be best if Little League players were between 9 and 12 years old, though we had no intention of excluding any precocious eight-year-old from playing. I was having a wonderful time becoming more and more involved in the evolution of the game.

I now had a plan and the rules were worked out, but there were still questions that kept coming up. Where was I going to get the money to finance a league of baseball teams for young boys? I struggled for weeks with that one simple but overriding question. It never occurred to me to throw in the towel, to concede defeat. Imagine having to go back and tell Jimmy and Major I couldn't do it, that I'd tried and failed!

The fact is, I had begun to think bigger, not smaller. I sat up one night composing a letter to a cereal company in Michigan extolling the merits of my program and how it could blossom into other athletic programs for kids during summer vacation. This was an idea ready for financial support.

I finally gave up writing for the night, unable to compose the right letter. In fact, I never did complete it. But, the idea of a variety of organized sports programs for kids stayed with me. That's why, when I designed the first emblem for Little League it was an eagle with LITTLE LEAGUE emblazoned on its outstretched wings and "Baseball for Boys" below. I hoped the same emblem could be used for activities that would include girls. I saw many possibilities for my daughter, Monya Lee, and her girlfriends as well as for boys who were not baseball players.

As the years came and went, I realized Little League baseball was all I could handle as a completely volunteer activity. By the time World War II had ended and Little League had begun to grow rapidly, I had put all thought of expanding into other realms far behind me. The closest I came to involvement in anything else but Little League was to encourage the founders of P.O.N.Y. League baseball for 13-to-15-year-olds. I regretted not being able to organize baseball for girls, but in the early forties I was so absorbed in Little League for boys that I didn't have time.

In 1942, our finances improved slightly soon after an elderly gentleman began attending the games at our field in Memorial Park. W. E. Villinger would drive up in his large, black coupe, take out a bentwood kitchen chair, and seat himself at sidewalk level to watch the kids play.

One day he brought along a special cup he had made by cutting down a tin fruit can. He had soldered a curved handle to it and gave it to a boy named Bobby Vaughn. Bobby was a heavyset boy who had tried out but couldn't make the team. Bobby passed the cup among the fans to collect contributions for the league. We found Bobby so valuable that eventually we gave him an official uniform and cap. He was a favorite with the fans, and with Mr. Villenger.

In 1944, Mr. Villenger invited me to meet with him at the Ross Hotel to hear a proposal he had for me. He wanted a living memorial to his daughter, who had died in childbirth some years before. He wanted to pay me to organize a baseball league for girls in his daughter's memory. He told me he thought the activity would help build up girls like his daughter and prevent their dying, prematurely, in childbirth.

Telling him I couldn't accept his offer was one of

the hardest things I ever had to do, for I knew his proposal was an act of pure love. Looking back on it, I wish I had had the time, wealth, and endurance to develop the variety of activities I had envisioned for both boys and girls. Had I attempted it under the circumstances, I fear even Little League would have died in infancy, for the parent would not have been able to give it the love and care it needed to thrive and grow during its formative years. At any rate, I reluctantly concluded that national sponsorship was out of the question and began to think about raising needed funds locally.

When I finally had a plan, I persuaded my close friend Chuck Heim to meet with me before work. As we sat in his car in front of Woolworth's, I tested my approach for soliciting prospective Little League sponsors. Since Chuck had never played organized baseball and wasn't even a fan, his sport being tennis, I knew he'd be objective. Though my spiel neither aroused his enthusiasm nor drew any criticism, I felt encouraged enough to proceed as I had planned.

Before the morning was over, I was making my first pitch. Timidly, I asked to speak to the owner of a local business. When I explained the nature of my visit, I got a polite refusal.

During the next two-and-a-half months I lost some of my timidity. As I made collections for Lundy Lumber Company, I also solicited sponsors for Little League. Though I wasn't exactly a smashing success, I did learn. Whenever I'd think of a prospect or a name was suggested, I'd jot it down in my notebook so that at the first opportunity I could make my pitch.

Although the response continued to be negative, I went ahead and ordered a dozen baseballs and a catcher's mask from a firm in Chicago. The cost of $3.67 plus 82 cents for postage showed me just how expensive it was going to be to outfit and equip three teams and reinforced my determination to find sponsors.

I kept looking. Ten prospects turned me down, then 10...20...40...50. I was discouraged, but I wasn't about to give up the hope that someone would be willing to put some money into organized baseball for boys.

When I stopped at Lycoming Dairy Farms early in April, my 57th call, to talk to Floyd Mutchler, I got an attentive ear. He asked a few questions and must have liked the answers, for he said, "We'll go along, for the boys." Though he told me he'd have to talk it over with his partner, H. R. Paulhamus, he assured me a check would be ready if I would return later in the week.

My persistence and faith in what I was doing had finally paid off. On April 13, Lycoming Dairy Farms became the first sponsor of Little League baseball.

I didn't waste any time putting their $30 check to use. The next day I bought two bats and a catcher's mitt. Then I added a pair of leg guards and four balls, each a different model from those I already had.

Though the dozen balls I had sent for were all the same, I knew I would have to test them against these four to determine which would hold up best. It didn't take long to decide that more-expensive, better-quality balls were what we needed. I concluded, too, that we would need a ball that was less lively than the official major-league balls. I thought the big-league balls would cover the distance between batter and infielders much too fast because of the pared-down size of the Little League diamond.

Exactly two weeks after I'd picked up the check from Lycoming Dairy Farms, I set out in search of uniforms.

At the Kresge 25¢-to-$1 store, I found one displayed on a mannequin. Priced at $1.29, it included socks. I bought one to test for size. The clerk agreed to check with the Kresge home office to see if the uniforms could be had in different colors. While I waited for an answer on the uniforms, I continued to buy equipment.

One of my calls was to a very busy neighborhood grocery, where I saw a large poster promoting a new bread package by Butter Krust Bakers. Several evenings later, the newspaper carried the same information in a half-page ad. The company was from Sunbury, about 40 miles down river. Since the Williamsport bakers had already refused to sponsor a team and the Sunbury firm was looking for a way to break into the local market, I decided it would be a good prospect.

A few days later, I took my wife, our 2-½-year-old daughter, and my mother-in-law for a late-afternoon spring-time ride. By the time we arrived in Sunbury, the manager had gone home, so I asked for directions and followed him, only to learn that he had returned to the bakery. About that time, I noticed my car engine wasn't running smoothly, but I returned to the bakery anyway. The manager promptly gave me a firm no. It was the unsettling kind of day that made me thankful just to arrive home without mishap.

It was soon after that I was out making a collection for Lundy's when I spotted a group of boys playing ball in a field. I parked my car and walked over to talk to them. I wanted to know if any of the men in the neighborhood ever came out to umpire their games or to coach them.

"Yeah, that man down on the corner," one of the boys replied, pointing.

As I approached the corner house, I immediately recognized the man hoeing in his garden. It was Dave

Kramer, one of my boyhood heroes. He had played third base on the Pennsylvania Railroad team in the early twenties.

I introduced myself and began explaining that I was looking for someone like him to organize a team of younger boys to play in the league I was trying to set up.

"That's a good idea," he conceded, "but between my job on the railroad, which calls me out at odd hours, and my bowling, I'm pretty busy. With my wife working, I think I should be spending a little more time at home. I don't believe I can take on another project right now."

As in other instances of initial rejection of my request, Dave's "no" wasn't for life. He later became active in Lincoln Little League, established in 1946, which played on a diamond directly across the street from his home.

My impulsive call on Dave Kramer was the first time I'd thought of looking for people who would be willing to accept full responsibility for a team, including financing. After all, since I was out looking for team sponsors, I might as well look for managers, too.

At the first opportunity, I called on George "Mac" Hoffnagle, who was in charge of a local boys' club. Though he was interested, his budget was too limited for him to squeeze out the money for equipment and uniforms, and I couldn't promise a sponsor to finance a team. I kept looking.

A newspaper article led me to another prospect, Ray "Lefty" Fedder, a city policeman. Lefty had been a NY-Penn League pitcher. The police department had decided to organize a junior baseball team to help alleviate the delinquency problem, and he had been recruited to manage the program. Though the department was only interested in working with older boys, I left reassured that there were others who believed in the character-building influence properly supervised baseball could have on boys.

A month passed after Lycoming Dairy gave me its check, and I still didn't have any other sponsors. But, I was positive that three was the minimum number of teams the league could operate with and still provide interesting competition. So, I ordered nine more uniforms from Kresge's, all the same color, and opened a $30 charge account at Harder's Sporting Goods Store. Harder's had a dozen uniforms on hand for $18 and was trying to locate another 10 in a different color. Although I had only one sponsor and one manager, me, I saw no turning back. It was time to begin calling boys together for team tryouts.

Chapter 4

Eager as I was to get boys to try out, I didn't want so many that I'd have to turn most of them away. That ruled out radio and newspaper announcements. I chose more modest means when I put out the call May 7 that I was ready to recruit. I invited the boys from the junior department of St. John's Lutheran Sunday School, where I was a member, to meet me under the tree outside after class. The meeting was so brief that we completed it before the worship service began. I told the boys about my plans for a baseball league and invited them to report the next evening at 6 o'clock at Max M. Brown Memorial Park.

I also told Major and Jimmy to spread the word to the boys that had been with us when I worked out the size of the diamond and to anybody else who might be interested.

Much as I would have liked to have all three of my nephews play, I could not. I thought Carl, 13, was too old to compete against the younger boys. I knew how disappointed he was and tried to ease his pain by having him assist me with the tryouts.

Monday was a beautiful spring day. That evening a good number of boys turned out at Memorial Park. All the boys who had been with me in 1938 were there along with eight from church and four who had gotten the word from their friends.

Carl, also known as Bud, had been thinking about how to communicate effectively with the boys. His thoughtfulness had led him to present me with a whistle attached to a braided lanyard he'd made.

"This'll get the kid's attention," he said. I still have it, along with everything else from those days.

After explaining what was expected, Bud and I paired the boys off to play catch, in groups of four, with the new balls I had purchased.

It was a good start, but I was still short two of the sponsors I needed, and the managers I absolutely had to have seemed nowhere to be found. The previous week, I talked to a few men who I thought might manage teams, but each turned me down. My wife, Grayce, shared my frustrations.

The next day Grayce told her friend and coworker Annabelle Bebble about the tryouts the night before and our dilemma. Annabelle suggested I ask her husband, George, to help, and Grayce and I invited them to our home.

Before the Bebbles arrived, I arranged on the sofa a display of the equipment I had purchased: the pinstriped uniform and socks on one end and the chest protector, mask, shin guards, catcher's mitt, two fielder's gloves, a partly-filled box of new balls, and a bat on the other. I was eager to create an atmosphere that would help George make up his mind.

It must have been right, because George accepted managership of a team after I explained my plans for the league. His acceptance would have to be conditional, though, since he played baseball on the Roaring Branch team in County League and would not always be available.

When I explained that I was still one manager short for a three-team league, George recommended his brother, Bert, also a member of the Roaring Branch team.

By the time I called on Bert, George had explained my plan for Little League. I had my third manager.

Bert remained an invaluable part of Little League for two-and-a-half years, until the middle of the 1941 season, when his employer changed his work schedule, making it impossible for him to work with the boys. I offered to talk to his boss, but he decided not to risk antagonizing his supervisor by seeking special consideration.

I was disappointed to lose such an effective volunteer as Bert had been. The boys loved him. He had become a real friend to many of them and their parents and fans. Fortunately, Merlin Edler, father of one of Bert's boys, volunteered when Bert approached him, agreeing to coach the team for the rest of the season.

George Bebble's participation lasted some two years longer than Bert's, ending when Uncle Sam intervened halfway through the 1943 season. Annabelle and George had spent many hours with their team and, like Bert, left a deep impression on many of the boys. George's letter of resignation, it turned out, was a bit premature, for like me, he'd been called but was never inducted. By then, however, we had named a replacement for him. George resumed managing a few years later, in another league. Some two decades later when I asked men who had played Little League baseball at its very beginning to share memories for the 25th Anniversary observance, one wrote:

> *I remember George Bebble. He looked like he was born with a baseball cap on and always had a bat in his hand.*

Now I was set. I had three teams and three managers. With the season opener just weeks away, we had to have a permanent playing field. I called on the Department of Parks and Public Property to get permission to build a field where we had been conducting tryouts. Aside from occasional softball games played by picnickers, that part of the park was seldom used.

Because our intention was to play hardball and not softball, my request was turned down by city council. The news was disappointing, but not disastrous, for the council offered an alternative I knew we could make work.

Our first Little League field was on the "sandlot" at Park Point. The Sunday School League had used the site years earlier and the dilapidated remains of the wood-and-wire-mesh backstop, which the city agreed to patch, were still there. So was the skinned infield; and it was good enough to use. Although left-center-field sloped away from the infield and the center- and right-field levels were low, it wasn't that much of a problem. The real problem lay in the fact that home plate faced directly into the setting sun. Definitely the wrong place for it to be for twilight play! I was sure we would be able to correct that problem, too. With some effort, we could turn the field 90 degrees to disarm the sun.

As we moved to our new location, we continued to test the ability of the boys to field ground balls, catch flies, throw, and bat. During that week, more and more boys were showing up to try out. By the time George, Bert, and I selected our squads, we had a pretty fair idea of everyone's skill level. With 24 boys to choose from, we had only eight players each. We decided to recruit two more 11- or 12-year-old players for each team.

At a field meeting, unattended by the boys, we considered each boy separately. When we were finished, we had distributed the talent as well as we could to make each unit competitive with the others. We gave the boys their predetermined assignments at the next practice session. Then each manager went to work molding his squad into a team.

At the end of the 24-game schedule, we couldn't have been more pleased with the results. The teams had records of 9-7, 8-8, and 7-9. The middle team won the five-game play-off series, 3-2. Our team balance had been better than any of us had dared hope when the season began. It was the best possible balance short of a three-way tie.

As we had begun the season, one dark cloud still hung over me. Although things were coming together and I had managers and players, a field and equipment, and umpires, I still hadn't come up with the other two sponsors I needed to help finance our operation.

I was more determined than ever to succeed when I stopped at the Penn Pretzel Company to make my pitch. As I stepped into the production room, Jesse Smith nodded to acknowledge my presence, indicating he would soon be with me. He was busy making pretzels. As the conveyor belt moved by, he picked up a length of dough, gave it a twist, and placed it on a screen-covered frame. When the supply of dough lengths was finally exhausted, I introduced myself and explained my purpose.

Probably to gain time to think about my request, he excused himself and picked up a number of the screened frames and carried them to another part of the room. By the time he returned, he had made a decision. He didn't give me a flat no, but indicated he wasn't able to put $30 into the project. He wasn't trying to bargain, for I sensed sympathy for my plans, so I made a compromise proposal.

"I've already bought equipment, ordered uniforms, and have boys trying out for the teams, so I must move quickly to prepare for the first game," I told him. "If you will pay only the cost of the caps and the sponsorship emblems, I'll be able to proceed."

"How much would that be?" Jesse Smith wanted to know.

"Eighteen dollars," I estimated.

If he could pay in two installments, he replied, he could handle that much. On a handshake, we agreed.

Now, with two sponsors, I did what I had been reluctant to do: I asked my boss to sponsor a team. As soon as Jack Lundy became aware that my project was baseball, he suggested, "Talk to Dick; he's the baseball man."

Dick Lundy listened patiently as I explained my vision of organized baseball for little boys and the progress I had made finding sponsors. I asked if he would object to my naming a squad the Lundy Lumber team. I suggested that once he saw us in operation he might want to make a contribution. To my great joy, he accepted. I went home to design team emblems.

Of the three original Little League sponsors, Lundy's support has lasted the longest. They are still supporters of Original Little League and numerous times have contributed far beyond the usual sponsorship fee. Lycoming Dairy Farms continued to sponsor a team until their 1966 merger with Dairylea. Penn Pretzel Company went out of business before the 1940 season began.

Because of the expense involved, I decided there were some items of equipment we simply couldn't afford to buy. Besides, some weren't available in the right sizes at any price. The alternative was obvious. I would have to make them myself.

First on my list was home plate. I had already decided the width across the front would be only 14-$\frac{1}{8}$-inches, narrow enough so that a small boy's bat could cover the full width when he swung at the ball.

If necessity is the mother of invention, knowing where to find materials one can adapt to specific needs must be a close relative. In this case, I remembered a sizable piece of half-inch-thick hard, black rubber that had been in my dad's basement for years. When I checked, it was still there.

Cutting the rubber was much more difficult than I'd anticipated, and I quickly found the paring knife I had was inadequate for the job. Fortunately, I had a tool at home I believed would cut through the exceedingly tough material. It was a brand-new pocketknife I'd been awarded for winning a foot race at a Pennsylvania Railroad Company picnic when I was a youngster.

On the walk to my house, I kept questioning the wisdom of using the pocketknife and possibly ruining a treasured keepsake. Mother Necessity dictated my decision, though, and I returned to Dad's house with the knife and went to work.

Even though I began at a corner and was able to get by with cutting only three sides, the job took a long time. Sharp blade notwithstanding, I broke it before I finished fashioning the plate. Actually, I found the half-length blade was an improved tool for the task at hand. I regretted the damage to my keepsake, but was pleased with my craftsmanship. I finished the job by making holes in the corners so we could spike the plate to the ground at game time and remove it when we were done.

Later I made a pitcher's rubber 18-inches long and four inches wide that also could be spiked in place. I painted both white.

Making bases presented more of a problem. I could design them, but I knew I needed help to put them together properly. I cut white duck, a canvaslike material, to a pattern, and my sister Laurabelle stitched the pieces together. I then had grommets placed in the two open edges so that we could lace heavy-duty twine through them to hold the bags together and keep the excelsior stuffing salvaged from a local drugstore from coming out.

To make sure the bases could be fastened securely, I cut strips of white duck and double-folded them to be stitched, making a strap to which I attached a buckle. The strap, attached to the bag, slipped through a long staple pushed into the ground at each base. Buckled, it kept the bag from moving out of position. When the bags became badly soiled and flattened, we could open them, remove the stuffing, and launder them to make them look like new.

With the first game only days away, I still had no name for the boys' league. That was the situation Saturday morning, June 3, when I made my first visit to the Williamsport Sun, the city's evening paper.

"Hiya, Tuck," said Bob Steinhipler, sports editor, as I approached his desk.

Bob, about two years my senior, and I had played ball together when we were both very young, so I found it easy to tell him about the new league. When I asked him to inform his readers of the opening game and publish the schedule for the first half of the season, he asked, "What's the name of the league?"

"I had been thinking of calling it Junior League Baseball until I remembered there's a woman's organization named "Junior League."

Actually, I wanted to pattern the name after the big leagues, as the major leagues were popularly referred to. So the idea of calling the organization Little League had occurred to me. But, I had reservations. I was afraid the people would think the name referred to the league rather than to the boys. I'd also thought of the name Little Boys' League and decided it didn't sound right.

The result was that I still hadn't made up my mind. Although I liked the sound of Little League, I needed more time to think about it. Bob agreed and told me to get back to him later in the morning.

From the offices of the *Sun*, I walked directly to *Grit*, the local Sunday paper. At *Grit*, I spoke to Bill Kehoe, a friendly man who was to become a good friend of mine and a booster of baseball for boys. Bill was *Grit's* sports editor.

Because I'd never met Bill before, I had to explain who I was and go into great detail about what I was trying to do. Bill listened attentively and asked only an occasional question. Eventually he asked the same question Bob had asked, "What is the name of the league?" After I explained what I had been thinking, he responded in favor of Little League. That settled the issue with me.

When I left the *Grit* offices, I phoned Bob with the name. That evening the *Sun* announced the first game for Little League. The next day Bill Kehoe mentioned the league in his *Grit* column, "Fodder for the Sports Fan," referring to it as "Tuck's Little League." A third item appeared in the morning *Gazette & Bulletin* announcing the new league's first game.

Though the name Little League was not exactly anchored in cement at that point, with these announcements it seemed pretty well set. My nickname preceding it quickly fell into disuse and we dropped it officially when we planned for the second season. The boys, however, continued to call *me* Tuck.

Chapter 5

No one who hasn't experienced it can imagine the first-time thrill of being issued a uniform one very much desires. The Little League uniform meant, simply, "You are a member of a team. You are a baseball player. You are somebody special."

The first time we issued uniforms was the easiest for the managers, for we had one for every player. No one was turned away; no one was disappointed. That was never the case in our league in later years.

All uniforms were the same size, but most boys from 8 to 12 could wear them. They had not come boxed or packaged, so we folded pants, socks, and cap into each shirt. The Lundy uniforms were steel gray. The shirts were trimmed with red and gold. Jumbo Pretzel's were cream-colored, with pinstripes and red trim. Lycoming's were pearl gray with blue trim. They were a lot like the big-leaguers'.

Although I can't remember the reactions of specific boys when they received their uniforms in 1939, I have distinct impressions of the types of reactions then and later.

With the suspense of the tryouts gone, some, wanting to appear casual, paused to ask a question or make a comment. Most, though, as they queued up in front of the manager, shifted their feet nervously, craning their necks to see the boys at the head of the line get their due. Some held the pants and shirt to their bodies, making a rough check on how well they might fit. Some turned around and ran toward home at top speed, eager to show their newest symbol of success to parents and family. Some acted as though getting the new uniform was an everyday occurrence and walked away nonchalantly, for about 50 feet, before giving vent to the excitement and dashing madly off the field.

That first year and in the years since, mothers of Little Leaguers have told me in various ways how much the uniform means to a small boy. "We couldn't get him to take it off." "He wanted to wear it to bed." "When I asked him to go to the store for me, he went upstairs and put on his uniform." "On game days he puts on his uniform right after lunch."

Whatever it means to small boys, seeing them in baseball uniforms has meant a great deal to me. During my years of travel around the country for Little League, I was frequently on the road at the time children were walking to country schools. Whenever I saw a boy with books, lunch box, ball glove, and wearing a baseball cap, I felt amply repaid for my efforts to help others like him get the chance to play under conditions suited to their size and ability. The uniform has been an important part of it.

June 6, 1939 was a great day. Just 10 months from the time I had made my spur-of-the-moment promise to Jimmy and Major, it was coming true. Little League baseball was born.

My Lycoming Dairy team, on which Jimmy and Major played, was the visiting team against George Bebble's Lundy Lumber team. It was a big game, begun without fanfare. There was no place for anyone to sit and watch, and there were few fans present. The excitement was mostly inside the managers and the players. The one park bench available served both teams when they were at bat.

After the Lundy team took the field, its infielders

made their practice pegs to first base and Frank Sipe, the pitcher, took his warmup tosses. Then, Harold Schleif, my brother-in-law, called, "Play ball!" from his umpiring position behind the pitcher.

Lycoming Dairy mounted a mild offensive and scored one run in the top of the first inning, the first run in Little League baseball. Its lead was short-lived, for Lundy Lumber struck back hard, scoring seven runs in its half of the inning.

Max Miller, Lycoming Dairy's pitcher, was doing an excellent job following my instructions to throw strikes to his catcher, Fred Sander. Unfortunately, the strikes seemed to be consistently where Lundy's batters liked them. Frank Sipe held Lycoming scoreless in the second and third innings, while his team scored eight runs in the bottom of the second. I knew the time to make some changes was at hand. I moved Miller to right field, Jimmy Gehron from right field to second base, and our left-hander, Major Gehron, from second base to the mound. Miller didn't pitch much after that, but became a dependable third baseman and outfielder for Lycoming Dairy.

The Lundy boys, not exactly overawed by the pitching change, quickly added four runs off Gehron. At the end of three innings, the score was a very lopsided 19-1.

With the game half over, the teams began playing a more-balanced brand of ball. Lycoming Dairy scored three runs in the fourth, three in the fifth, and one in the sixth, while holding Lundy Lumber to two runs in the fourth and two in the fifth. Lycoming Dairy had regained its composure and outscored Lundy Lumber 7-4 in the last three innings, but it was a case of too little, too late. The final score of 23-8 was the highest of the season.

Once the season opener was out of the way, the

boys played a lot of closely competitive baseball. Lycoming took the first-half crown with a 5-3 won-loss record but fell to third place in the second half with a 3-5 record. Lundy's, second in the first half at 4-4, came in first in the second half with five wins and three losses. Jumbo, winning three games for third place the first half, won four to finish second the second half.

Eight of the 24 games were won by a single run; five, by two runs. In only seven games was the margin of victory more than four runs.

One fact we were proud of at the end of the season was that only four games after the first produced scores in double digits, and on each occasion only for the winning team. The comparatively low scores and the closeness of most of them kept the outcome of many of the games unpredictable up to the last out. The suspense made the games and the season exciting and enjoyable for the managers as well as for the boys. It stimulated us to look eagerly toward another season.

However glowing the 1939 season was, I had no idea at the time what an exciting and overall satisfying life that first Little League baseball game would lead to. I was too busy trying to resolve problems that kept popping up with almost every move we made to think very far into the future.

Late-spring rains caused postponements of games 2, 3, and 5, scheduled for June 8, 13, and 20. All we could do was wait and hope for better weather. As so often happens with unforeseen setbacks, the rain postponements were not the detriments they seemed. In retrospect, it is clear that they materially affected the entire course of Little League history for the better. Exposing playing-field problems we hadn't been aware of, the effects of the rains pushed us into remedial action we wouldn't have gotten around to so soon, if at all, had we had nothing but fair weather.

During the late-afternoon downpour on June 8, for example, big cinder clinkers washed onto the infield from the slightly higher abandoned trolley-car roadbed nearby. Looking at the field on my way home from work, I decided if we worked quickly we would still be able to play that night. So instead of sitting down to supper, I hurried to the field with equipment and bushel basket in hand. Borrowing a rake, we removed the cinders and smoothed the area around third base where the rain had formed a shallow ditch that drained into the outfield. Bert put down the bases and I got the pitcher's rubber and home plate in place in time for play.

Despite our high hopes, just as we were about to start the game, a heavy shower sent us running for cover and forced us to postpone it. When Mother Nature finally relented and permitted us to play again, it was June 15.

I had arrived early to begin preparing the field for the league's second game. I had just put down home plate, limed the base lines, and was installing the pitcher's rubber when several carloads of young men pulled up, got out, and began warming up with softballs.

I told one of them that the field was reserved for Little League that evening. He relayed my message to the others. That brought his entire group around me for a full-blown, rough-talk conference at the pitcher's mound.

Because of the shortage of playing fields, they used this one to make up rained-out games, they said, informing me they had one scheduled for that evening and intended to play it. They didn't seem impressed when I told them the Department of Parks had given Little League use of the field. In fact, several threatened to eject me.

Some of the uniformed Little Leaguers began arriving at this point for pregame warmup. Their presence made a stronger impression than anything I had said, and one of the cooler heads among the softball players suggested that perhaps they should find a field elsewhere. It was clearly because of the Little Leaguers that they left in good humor.

Shortly thereafter, George and Bert Bebble arrived and our second game was soon underway. Lundy Lumber defeated Jumbo Pretzel, 11-5.

Now Jumbo and Lycoming had each played one game; Lundy's had played two. The league was really on its way.

However, problems exposed by the rain would not go away. After the third of our first five games had to be postponed, I was convinced we couldn't easily improve field conditions. The only sensible alternative was to look for a better site for future seasons.

I was determined to make baseball as enjoyable an experience as I could for the boys, so during the second week of the season, I took uniformed Little Leaguers to Bowman Field for a practice session with the Williamsport Grays. I had hoped that each boy would be able to spend some time with his counterpart on the Grays. I figured the boys could learn some of the fundamentals of their positions from the professionals better than they could from me or the other managers.

I was disappointed for the boys when the Grays' manager vetoed the idea. He thought the boys were too young to understand, though he did designate Sam Page, one of his pitchers, to talk to them a little about pitching. Every professional had an aura of greatness in the eyes of baseball-loving little boys at that time, and our boys were no different. It was a wonderful experience for them. I hoped it would motivate them to do their very best on the diamond and help them enjoy the game more.

That first season we usually had only one umpire for each game. He called balls, strikes, and plays at the bases. Like the managers, the umpires were unpaid volunteers.

At a game late in June, a fan standing along the first-base line noisily berated the umpire for what he insisted was a bad strike call. The umpire said nothing; he simply walked off the field and positioned himself among the spectators.

Without an umpire, the game could not continue. I went to the mound to address the spectators in defense of all the umpires who volunteered their time to us. I explained that the game was for the kids. Our desire in Little League, I said, was to establish conditions as much like those in the big leagues as possible except baiting the umpires and riding opposition players. I concluded by asking the fans' cooperation.

Needing an umpire so the game could continue, I asked for someone in the crowd to volunteer. Larry King, a fellow employee at Lundy's, stepped forward, and the fans applauded. Larry worked the rest of the game without incident.

This episode was an early indicator of the nature of problems over-zealous fans can cause. We always tried to anticipate such disruptions so we would be ready to check them when they occurred. Nine men umpired for Little League in 1939, some continued for many years.

Despite our field and money problems, when games weren't being rained out, the play was exciting and good. Parents and friends turned out to cheer the boys on, stimulating pride in their good plays and encouraging them to practice all the harder to improve. The program was quickly justifying its existence.

After the third inning of the July 6 game, I introduced a new way to raise money for the league. Standing on the mound and holding a hollow rubber ball about the size of a baseball for all the fans to see, I explained that although the sponsors' contributions paid a big part of the cost of equipment, we needed additional support to pay other expenses. I thanked them for being there, then showed them that the top third of the ball had been cut away, making it a receptacle. I said I would place it on the ground at a corner of the backstop so that anyone who wished could contribute to Little League. We collected $1.42 that day. That hollow rubber ball became a regular part of future games.

I was also talking about a new field with George and Bert. Were they committed enough to the program to share in the effort to build our own special Little League field if we found the right location? Yes, they answered, and we began the search. Our goal was to provide the finest baseball field for boys anywhere. The Little League dream just kept growing.

Because we wanted to keep the field within walking or cycling distance of each player's home, we confined the search for a new site to the residential area around the park, where a sizable vacant lot seemed impossible to find. That required us to think about what might be and not let our vision be clouded by what was. Without that philosophy, I might never have thought of turning the site at the corner of Memorial Avenue and Demorest Street into a baseball field.

I passed this site every time I drove to a game. It was

enclosed by a heavy-wire-mesh fence about seven feet high and included a wooded section, an old tennis court that was overgrown with underbrush, a long, six-foot-high concrete retaining wall, and a parking lot for the nearby-warehouse employees. It wasn't very appealing to look at, but I thought its location and the fact that it was enclosed made it a good possibility.

I checked out the site as best I could before telling anybody about it. Because it was a corner lot, I stepped it off in each direction and decided it was about the right size if we laid out the field at a slight angle. The presence of two-story houses and tall trees on the west side of Demorest Street were a further advantage, for they would provide protection from the sun's glare during late-afternoon games.

First I talked it over with George and Bert and then went to the Dean Phipps Warehouse office to ask for the use of the land. As it turned out, the land didn't belong to the Phipps Company, but to the Williamsport Textile Company, across the street from the field.

Arthur Markgraf, plant superintendent, liked my proposal and promised to pass on my request to the home office.

That July my brother Ralph and his family came to visit with us from Naugatuck, Connecticut. He and his son, Ralph, Jr., immediately became immersed in Little League baseball.

Because we only had 10 players on a team and absences made substitutes necessary, Ralph, Jr., got to play in seven games before his vacation ended. He played in five games for Lycoming and one each for Jumbo and Lundy's. He is the only person who played on all three teams of the first Little League.

When all 10 players on the roster were present, we

used four outfielders that first season because we didn't like the idea of a lone player sitting on the bench while the others were in the field. When one was going to be away for a game, he would tell his manager and return his uniform so that a substitute player could use it. He got his uniform and place on the team back when he returned.

That summer Ralph had a host of fans rooting for him, including his grandparents. They showed up to cheer for him and their other Little Leaguer grandsons, Major and Jimmy. In later years, they saw two more grandsons play Little League Baseball, though it took a trip to Tennessee.

As a boy reared on his uncle's farm, my dad had experienced a crude game played with a yarn ball at recess on a side-hill country school-yard. He became an avid baseball fan as he grew up, and when he had sons of his own, he liked to have one of them with him at games.

Dad was an employee of the Pennsylvania Railroad and, despite his modest means, was rich in travel opportunities, for he had a railroad pass. His pass, a lunch bag of chicken sandwiches, and $1.10 bleacher tickets took us to New York and Washington for major-league games. We'd leave Williamsport by coach at 1:10 a.m. and return about the same time the following morning. I still have six rain checks from games called in the midtwenties.

Together Dad, my brother, and I watched such diamond stars as Tris Speaker, Ty Cobb, Max Carey, Walter Johnson, Babe Ruth, Lou Gehrig, Grover "Pete" Alexander, Joe Dimaggio, and many other greats of the game.

At times, Dad would tell Harold (Whitey), my brother, and me about his plans in advance, encouraging us to pass the word to some of our friends whose fathers had railroad passes, too. However many responded, Dad was usually the only adult in the group, and happy about it.

Perhaps this sharing of his great interest in baseball was the impetus, the subconscious influence, that led me to say on many later occasions that ""Little League makes dads of fathers."

Ralph's experiences with Dad were similar to mine, and it was reflected in his and Ralph, Jr's avid interest in playing at every opportunity that summer. When we got the good news that the Williamsport Textile lot was ours to turn into a baseball diamond for Little League, Ralph volunteered the use of his old Hudson to uproot the smaller trees. We hooked one end of a heavy chain to the car and the other to a tree, which the powerful old Hudson would pull right out of the ground.

Monday, Wednesday, and Friday of the next week we continued removing brush and small trees. We asked the players to help. They dragged the branches and piled them up for later disposal. They also pulled small sumac trees and thorny vines from the ground. It was one of the Little League events remembered by some of the "boys" at the 25th Anniversary celebration.

Once the small stuff was out of the way, Ralph and I felled the remaining trees with a crosscut saw and ax, and the boys continued piling up branches. As he had promised, Mr. Markgraf had Howard Shooter and his maintenance crew remove the stumps of the larger trees.

I often wondered why Ralph would have subjected his car to such heavy work while he was almost 300 miles from home. I believe that in seeing Ralph, Jr., and me totally absorbed in Little League he was simply swept up in our enthusiasm. He was a great man, with such altruism marking the course of his life. In 1949, he was the moving force in establishing a Little League in Naugatuck and building a beautiful field, complete with large clubhouse, shower room, and other first-class accessories. It was the first field in New England built especially for Little League. Once that project was out of the way, Ralph became deeply involved in the Babe Ruth League in Naugatuck and organized a boys' band.

Ralph was one of many hundreds of men throughout Little League deserving of special thanks for their exceptional contributions to the game. Millions of Little Leaguers have benefited from their efforts, and many have been motivated by such examples to give of themselves.

As the summer wore on, our Little League boys were becoming mini-celebrities as their pictures and accounts of the games showed up in the local papers.

By then the boys had already played an abbreviated exhibition game at Bowman Field, as guests of the Grays, before an Eastern League game. It was an even bigger thrill to play another exhibition game that August as an added attraction for "Bicycle and Suburban Night." Through these games Little League got exposure far beyond Williamsport, for Eastern League baseball drew fans from a wide area.

The local papers covered the story, urging fans to see the "youngest known organized baseball players in this section of the country" capable of playing an advanced game of ball.

Among the best friends Little League had that first season were the local sports editors and writers. They reported virtually every game, complete with box and line scores and batting, pitching, and fielding summaries. Their enthusiasm for what Little League and Little-Leaguers were doing was one of the sparks that was to set the entire community ablaze with excitement for small-boy baseball. The power of the press in this instance was well used.

The press raves so early in Little League's existence

were like high-powered vitamins, and the boys, George, Bert, and I were overjoyed with them. We couldn't have agreed more with Bob Steinhelper's accolade describing Little League as the best thing that has happened around here in a long time.

When the Grays announced the 75th Anniversary celebration of baseball in Williamsport to be commemorated August 23-29 at Bowman Field, I was named to the pageant committee as the representative of Little League, one of the numerous baseball organizations to participate. We were now an accepted part of the local sports community.

With acquisition and the clearing of the plot at Memorial Avenue and Demorest Street, a new era began for Little League, and for me. I was constantly reviewing the various aspects of our experience with Little League since the introduction of player candidates to the game on May 8. I was determined to find a way to assure that Little League would continue indefinitely. The immediate problem was to have the playing field ready for the first game of the 1940 season. I could deal with other problems over the winter.

Removal of the tree stumps in the tennis-court area revealed cinder fill just below the surface. It made sense to leave the cinders to improve drainage in the areas that would eventually be skinned for the base paths and infield play between the bases. Where we intended to sow grass, we sifted the cinders from the soil.

We all had the same goal: a neatly trimmed grass infield, with fielders in position, the pitcher on the mound, a batter in the box, and an umpire calling "Play ball!" To reach that goal, we all had a lot of work to do.

The future outfield had a sparse growth of sumac.

Ground-level weeds, including trailing briars, were certain to trip outfielders unless they were removed. All kinds of trash next to the large retaining wall had to be hauled away, and topsoil had to be brought in to raise the skinned area to the grade of the grassed area and provide drainage. Once that was done, we would have to plow and rake the grassed area of the infield before we could seed it.

Using a mason's line and stakes, I established and marked the various finish grades in amateur fashion. Then came the day when I wished I could remember how to find the hypotenuse of a right triangle. Fortunately, another family member was there to show me. My brother-in-law, Henry Gehron, helped me out, and I finished laying out the field.

After two weeks of mostly sifting cinders and grass roots from the soil in fair territory along the first-base line, I took a vacation with my family. We traveled to New York and took in the World's Fair and Jones Beach. Severe cases of sunburn sent us packing home again before the end of the week.

While we were out of town, Lewie Browne managed my Lycoming Dairy team to a 6-4 victory over Jumbo. Lewie not only substituted as manager for each of the three teams, he also umpired a number of games for us that year. I tried to get him to take on a team of his own for the 1940 season, but he was too involved with Boy Scouts to take on full-time activity with Little League.

By the end of the summer we were ready for fill and had two truck-loads brought in, later adding two loads of topsoil. We then got busy hand-raking the loose topsoil to the proper grade.

Things at the field came to a halt while we became totally absorbed in the five-game championship series, between September 5 and 19, pitting Lycoming Dairy, winner of the first half, and Lundy Lumber, winner of the second half against each other. Four consecutive rainouts prolonged the suspense until, finally, on the nineteenth, Lycoming won its third game, taking the series three games to two. The batters had really come alive for the playoff. The winning scores were 4-1, 12-3, and 18-5 for Lycoming and 9-4 and 13-5 for Lundy's. Their regular-season batting averages had been .259 for Lundy's and .249 for Lycoming, and .240 for Jumbo. It had been quite a summer, for all of us!

Immediately after the championship series ended, I moved full speed ahead to prepare the league banquet. Acting as toastmaster, I introduced Lewie Browne and the other managers, and our guest speaker, Thomas H. Richardson, president of the Eastern League. Tommy later gave out miniature baseballs, replicas of those used in the Eastern League, to all of the boys, who gave Tommy and their managers and sponsors team photos.

The local papers once again responded with full coverage of the event. Little League was becoming important to the city.

Forty years later, in 1979, an antique dealer's ad in the New York Times offered numbered limited-edition copies of pictures of the three first-season teams for $25. They were reprints of the photos I had matted and framed the afternoon of the banquet as a gift for Tommy Richardson for his support of the league and for sponsoring the banquet. What a surprise that was to me!

With the banquet behind us, construction of the new playing field became my top priority.

The felled trees and the huge pile of brush the boys had dragged together had to go, so under supervision of the local fire department we had an enormous bonfire, almost a celebration of the past season and seasons to come.

Once the final hand-grading of the infield was completed, I bought a special mix of grass seed to sow later. I also drove in 16 five-foot steel posts spaced evenly around the edge of the grassed part of the infield and, to keep people off it, strung 440 yards of two-point barbed wire. The posts and barbed wire remained in place until a few days before the 1940 season opened, when I brought in a heavy roller to compact the soil. Since we were able to conduct tryouts at our old site, there was no urgency to have things done early in the summer.

We were fortunate not to have to change the original ground level along the third-base line or in the outfield. But the soil at home plate, the pitcher's mound, and foul territory on the first-base side still needed to be sifted free of cinders, and the area in foul territory still needed to be seeded. I was concerned that the batter's box be just right for our little players.

For some time, I had been searching for clay or heavy soil to be used at home plate. I remembered how frustrating it had been for me as a boy to find a comfortable position at the plate. The batter's box always had two long depressions, sometimes 1-½ to 2-inches deep. I believed adding clay would keep that condition from developing for our Little Leaguers.

I finally found what I was looking for at a local construction site and had a truckload delivered to the field. I thought that solved the problem, but as the 1940 season got underway, it became apparent that clay was not the answer. It became too hard for sliding. So I replaced the clay with a mixture of sand and loam. So far as I know, that's still the best mixture to use at home plate and for the pitcher's mound when the players aren't using steel-cleated shoes.

At the end of the season, I accepted invitations to speak that would never have been extended had I not started Little League. I was one of several who addressed the local Rotary Club on "activities to prevent boys from becoming delinquents." I spoke at another club as the organizer of Little League. I was eager and happy to talk to them about the challenge and excitement I found in helping small boys play baseball.

The influence of Little League was also felt in local churches. One pastor described Little League as "the greatest remedy for juvenile delinquency ever discovered in this city."

What belonging to Little League meant to the boys is probably best illustrated by an event that occurred after that season ended. One of the youngest players from the Lundy team, eight-year-old Bobby Smith, had lost his left eye after he was hit by a dart. While he was convalescing in the hospital, his teammates sent him a picture of the team. Bobby's nurses told the newspaper that he prized the picture more than anything else he'd received after the accident. He would proudly show it, pointing out each of his teammates by name to anyone interested enough to pause by his bed. Bobby wouldn't have been without friends had there been no Little League, but through Little League *he had more close friends who had a common interest, and it showed.*

Chapter 6

A telephone call as the 1939 season came to a close pointed up the need for clearly defined rules regarding player eligibility that we could enforce fairly. Tommy Richardson was on the line. A friend wanted him to intercede with me to make sure his son could play in the league next season. When I was told where the boy lived, I explained that we would be establishing definite boundaries for all future seasons. If the boy lived within the boundaries, he would receive an application form inviting him to try out for the league.

Since, in this case, I knew the boy wouldn't qualify by residence, I suggested Tommy encourage the boy's father to interest other fathers in the neighborhood to form a league there. I offered to meet with them to explain Little League and answer their questions.

Tommy's call wasn't unique. A number of fathers in other sections of the city had called with similar requests.

I believed the fairest system would be one that would provide an opportunity for boys who played together at school or in the same neighborhood to play together on the baseball diamond. That's why, when the final plans were drawn up, we settled on established school-attendance boundaries to set residency requirements. Parochial-school pupils who attended schools outside these boundaries but lived within them were eligible, too. Initially, until more leagues were formed, boys in adjacent districts could only look, and wish adults in their districts would form teams for them.

Sometimes we had to disqualify boys. For example,

in 1947 a boy showed up at tryouts without an application. He gave an address with which I was familiar. Other boys from that same address had played for me before. Surprised that his last name was different, I said I thought Strykers lived at that address.

"Yes " he conceded. "Mrs. Stryker's my aunt."

As it turned out, he was visiting from his home on Long Island, New York, for the summer. That being the case, we did not allow him to try out since it could have kept a boy who lived in the neighborhood from being selected to play. Strict application of boundary requirements has been a continuing policy of Original Little League, though it has sometimes left emotional bruises with both the disqualified and the disqualifier. In this case, however, the boy did finally get a chance to play, in 1948. He was properly enrolled in a local school, as verified by the principal. Established residence within the district made him eligible, and provided a happy ending to his determined effort to become a Little League player.

Clearly established league boundaries and strict enforcement are as important now as they were then. By limiting the number of boys eligible to try out for teams, Little League expands the possibility that a given candidate will qualify for a position. If a league territory has twice as many eligible candidates as it can use, then the desirable procedure is to set more-restrictive boundaries and form a second league, making it possible for all the boys to play.

Residency wasn't the only requirement, aside from playing ability. To be accepted in the league, a boy also had to be of the right age.

In 1938, the boys I took to Memorial Park were quite young. Jimmy and Major Gehron were six and eight, respectively. The others were all friends of theirs and about the same age. George and Charles Fortner were six and eight; Raymond Best was eight; George and Stanley Keys were nine-year-old twins; and Robert, James, and Charles "Noonie" Smith were seven, nine, and eleven. When these boys were joined in 1939 by the older boys after the Sunday-school announcement, it quickly became obvious that in future seasons definite age limits would have to be set.

The league rules I roughed out for the managers to consider over the winter proposed that each team have 12 uniformed players and up to six reserve substitutes whose names would be registered with the league president, that no team have more than five uniformed 12-year-olds or fewer than three 10 years old or younger, and that no reserve substitute be played until all regulars had played at least three innings.

For six evenings over a period of weeks in January and February, we discussed the league constitution and rules I proposed until all of us understood and accepted the provisions they contained.

Since we had committed ourselves to fielding a fourth team for 1940, I began the search for a manager. Though it wasn't nearly as frustrating this time around, it did take some persistence, for the new manager did not come without persuasion, nor did I find him unassisted. Recruiting managers, even after Little League became an international institution, was seldom easy. In this instance, we had the fourth team's sponsor long before we had the manager.

As emcee when the three Little League teams appeared at Bowman Field in 1939, Tommy Richardson, who owned Richardson Buick, had publicly invited me to see him about sponsoring a team for 1940. Shortly thereafter, Harry Stein, owner of a local service station, sent a similar message.

When I learned that Jumbo Pretzel Company had gone out of business early in 1940, I contacted Mr. Stein and accepted $25 as payment toward sponsorship of a new team. He agreed to send the balance of the sponsorship fee once we had set it. Richardson Buick would replace Jumbo Pretzel. We had contracts drawn up and were ready to make final plans for the new season.

I was relieved to have a full sponsor for each team and the fees in hand or available upon request. I had raised $174.63 for the first season in 1939. Our plans for the 1940 season required considerably more money. The board budgeted $260 at its March 22 meeting. We were optimistic, for in spite of all the difficulties of the previous year, we had a deficit of only $36.72 at the end of the season. I kept injecting personal funds until the league was finally able to repay me in 1943, our first year in the black.

As I thought about a fourth manager, I knew he couldn't be just anybody. He had to be someone who would understand the full involvement expected of him and could be relied upon to give it.

Howard Gair, who had umpired the final game of the championship series in 1939, seemed a good prospect. He had been an umpire in the Sunday School League during my playing days 12 years earlier. Unfortunately, he couldn't fit into our early-season schedule. He was committed to umpiring all Penn State University's home games.

However, as an expression of interest in Little League, Howard volunteered to umpire for us whenever he could. That amounted to only four games in 1940, but an incredible 495 more over the next 15 years. He also trained his son, Vance, to umpire. Vance handled one game in 1940, 30 in 1941, and 21 in 1942 before he left for three years in the United States Navy. When he returned in 1946, he resumed umpiring for Little League, officiating in 637 games before he retired in 1967.

When Howard turned me down, I asked him for suggestions. He named John Lindemuth. John was a few years older than I, but I had known him admiringly at a distance in high school. He was the track star and I the underclassman trying hard to make the team. To the unstarlike performances of novice runners like me, the coach would growl, "What's the matter with you fellows? I'll put Johnny Lindemuth against you at any distance from the 100 to the half-mile and he'll beat every one of you. Now let's get the lead out!"

The closest I could ever get to Johnny was to feel the sting of the cinders flying off his spikes. Now Little League was going to bring us together in a way that was mutually more satisfying.

When I arrived at his home, he ushered me into his living room. It was like stepping back in time to colonial America. When he invited me to sit down, I chose a comfortable old rocker. As I reviewed the Little League adventures of the past season, Johnny seemed to become increasingly interested. I outlined some of the plans for the future and emphasized the league's need for a man interested in boys and baseball, one who would put in many hours to help provide the finest playing field in Pennsylvania.

My case stated, I relaxed a bit and started rocking as I asked him to think the proposition over and let me know his decision. At that, he frowned, and I was certain he was going to turn me down.

John then rose from his chair. Assuming he was

preparing to dismiss me, I rose too. But, to my astonishment and pleasure, he said he'd really like to manage a team and I could count on him.

When I expressed my appreciation, I told him I'd been sure he was going to turn me down when he frowned.

"Oh," hc said, "everything's all right now. I was just worried a little when you started rocking. You see, that's Peggy's favorite antique and we seldom sit on it."

I was really relieved, relieved he had accepted and relieved I hadn't broken the chair.

With Johnny's commitment in hand, I invited him and his wife to join Bert and George and me and our wives March 7 at our next planning meeting. That meeting turned out to be a very important milestone, for the solid foundation for everything that followed was put in place then. It was the "first official meeting" of the Little League Board of Directors, composed of all the team managers.

Although Johnny and Peggy were unable to attend this meeting, I announced his appointment as manager of the fourth team. George, Bert, and I declared the constitution and the rules of the organization "to be known as LITTLE LEAGUE" to be in effect for 1940. With that done, we appointed our wives, Annabelle, Eloise, and Grayce, to the board of directors. Then we all signed the constitution. Johnny and Peggy signed it at our next meeting, March 22.

We sought to arrange a smooth entry into the 1940 season. We were concerned that each team have a set pitching staff. To insure it, we added this rule: "Each team shall have registered with the Board of Directors four members eligible to perform the pitching duties during league games. No player other than a registered pitcher shall be allowed to pitch. The Board of Directors by vote may allow a team to withdraw from the registered pitchers' list any player the manager may choose and may approve the appointment of another player as a registered pitcher."

The pitching rule was well thought out and debated among us. It took much of the three hours of our March 7 meeting to come up with what we all agreed was a sound rule.

When I presented my budget of $260 in expenditures for the year, the board approved it and authorized me to be league purchasing agent. That enabled me to get moving early. My first task was to order four dozen uniforms of the same quality we had in 1939. I'd had a hard time getting uniforms the year before, so I was grateful for an early start. Harder's accepted my order and was eventually able to assure me that three dozen uniforms were coming from one company and a dozen from another.

Why so much trouble getting uniforms? Because World War II was spreading in Europe and our government, preparing for possible involvement, was purchasing huge amounts of uniform material and sporting-goods items for use in military-training camps. That left little boys' uniforms in short supply. War-caused shortages were to keep the spread of Little League in check for seven years. When the war was finally over, organized baseball for little boys spread as spectacularly as starbursts exploding on the Fourth of July.

Once the uniforms were in hand, we made another improvement. In 1939, team emblems had to be removed each time the uniforms were laundered, because they were made of wool felt. To avoid this, I decided the team name should be embroidered on each shirt and a letter on each cap. Again, I had help. Christina Lapka, a local seamstress, embroidered each of the four dozen uniforms and caps for us in time for the opening of the season.

Not quite certain how we would conduct the 1940 tryouts, we agreed only to call the boys for the first practice session. At that time we'd determine their ages and choices of position and decide how to proceed from there.

Conscious of the many rain-caused postponements in 1939, we decided to schedule nine games for the first half of the season and 9 or 12 for the second half, depending on the number of postponements in the first half. We also decided to play each Monday, Tuesday, Thursday, and Friday, to have a gala celebration at the opening game, June 3, and to find backups for team managers.

All of us knew there was a lot of work to be done before the new field would be ready for use. So we agreed to divide the responsibility for it four ways, then drew slips to see what each manager had to do to get the job done.

We also agreed that the best way to announce the first call for player candidates was to distribute a mimeographed letter to parents through the schools. The letter would specify time and place of the first tryout session, announce showing of *Touching All Bases*, the American Legion film, and provide a form for parents to fill in pertinent information we'd need for each boy. I quickly got busy and wrote the letter and took it to the schools.

Newspaper coverage and word of mouth was building interest in Little League in and around Williamsport. Boys outside our boundaries longed for the opportunity to play in a uniformed league, too.

Three boys from the Vallamont Park area in the north-central part of the city decided to do something about their desire to play. On a Friday evening in May, they walked about two miles to Memorial Park to talk to me.

Although I had to turn them down, I didn't want to

discourage them, so I explained our boundaries and how we enforced them and that we could only accommodate four teams on our field. They ought to talk to their fathers about starting a league in their own neighborhood, I told them.

The next day Merrill Winner, president of Neyhart's Hardware Company in Williamsport, called me to tell me that three boys were in his office asking him to sponsor a team and had referred him to me for further information. Mr. Winner said he was willing to sponsor the boys but didn't know where to find uniforms. I offered him 10 of our 1939 uniforms at 50 cents apiece. Soon after that, the boys came to my house to pick them up. I was every bit as excited about the transaction as they were.

It wasn't long before the boys came around again for 10 more uniforms. On their own, they had formed two teams that played each other all that summer. Being mostly 12-year-olds, they were able to move into the newly formed Intermediate League the next season. Hugh Bubb, Jr.'s father became a manager and served many years in that league. His boy had led the way.

Another of the boys in the two-team league was Dick Welteroth, who went on to become a pitcher for the Washington Senators in the 1950's. Had Dick lived within the prescribed boundaries, he would have become the first Little Leaguer to make the majors. As it was, though, Little League had provided the encouragement needed.

One of the 1938 "experimental"-team players, Charles "Pete" Fortner, also sought a career in baseball. Pete played second base for Lundy Lumber in 1939 and 1940. Later, he played on New York Yankee farm teams in Texas before moving on to other pursuits.

Others who played Little League in the early years

and went on to play professionally were Al Yearick, Art Getgen, Bud Rich, Bill Witmer, and Frank Beattie.

Despite our planning in March and April, when opening day of the 1940 season was only a week away, the field was still in no condition for games. We needed more fill, and the trash behind the retaining wall still lay there as unsightly as ever.

At that point, George, Bert, and I put on a crash program to get the field ready. Using a rented truck, we hauled fill provided by the Williamsport Water Company. With garden spades we hand-loaded that truck four times. Using garden rakes, George and Bert leveled it to the proper grade on the skinned part of the infield.

Before the week was out, I rented another truck and hauled the trash to the dump. With the purchase and use of a real luxury item, a new foul-line marker, the field was finally ready for the 1940 season opener.

During the energetic preseason effort to get the field ready, I met the most faithful and loyal person I have ever known, William F. "Mac" McCloskey.

Mac was not a man who would impress one with his stature, but he grew on me as I first became aware of his steady character and unremitting quest for excellence. I first saw him at league tryouts, watching intently but saying little. His posture was distinctive, for he usually stood with right arm across his heart, elbow cradled in his left hand, puffing occasionally on his ever-present pipe.

Mac's son, Dalton, had tried out and won a pitcher's spot on the expansion team. Mac showed up regularly at his son's games, quietly and imperturbably watching every play. He was far from impassive, though.

On his own, Mac bought balls, a catcher's mitt, made a Little League-regulation-size home plate, and caught

Dalton's practice pitches. Since their practice site was a ways from their home, they'd hike to and from it together, regularly.

Mac also bought a chest protector, shin guards, and a mask for the boys to use during practices unsupervised by Little League.

This very special man became officially involved in Little League in an emergency situation. On August 20, 1940, Clair Smith, who had been scoring the games, was absent, and Mac was asked to fill in. That was the start of an incredible record, for Mac scored every league game thereafter over a period of 28 years. That's 1,327 consecutive games! In addition, starting with the first Little League tournament in 1947, he scored all tournament games, both state and national, played on Original Little League Field. He arranged to take his annual vacation during those weeks so he would be available.

At the close of the 1940 season, having scored all the remaining games, Mac prepared cards listing each player's batting record. Each year thereafter through 1967, he prepared a card for every player for each year he played.

Mac's trustworthiness and careful attention to detail made him a natural for league treasurer, a position he later assumed and held until he asked to be relieved of it. When he gave up that job, he continued as a league trustee.

In the seventies, Original Little League's managing personnel established an annual postseason series in his honor. They called it the Mac McCloskey Tournament. It is still played annually.

Mac's wife, Helen, though not as deeply involved as Mac, supported him enthusiastically in his Little League activities. She worked with wives of other league personnel operating the concession stands for state and national tournaments, which became part of Little League before the forties ended. She prepared the barbecue which ended up in thousands of sandwiches during the series.

When their son, Dalton, grew up and found a bride, Mac and Helen first checked the Little League schedule, to avoid a conflict between a game and the wedding. They were truly dedicated to Little League.

Chapter 7

Managers as well as players were excited as we began the 1940 season June 3. We had devised a way for all the boys to participate in the opening ceremony. They would then make their 1940 playing debut in two three-inning exhibition games. That year it was Lundy's over Lycoming Dairy, 3-2, and Buick over Stein's by the same score.

The four 12-player teams had been selected from 77 candidates. The 29 who were not selected were assigned to the farm system we had set up to insure the younger boys a chance to play. Most of the minor-leaguers were also on the reserve-substitute lists. The three youngest players on the regular teams also played in the minor league. The minor league operated with 41 players that year. To try to insure that the team we added in 1940 would be competitive, I devised a player-selection system which included a player auction. The system has stood the test of many years in the leagues which adopted it. However, it never became a required Little League procedure so long as franchised leagues had adopted an acceptable alternative.

My system allotted 20,000 points to each manager. Managers then established the value of each returning team member. The points spent for those players were deducted from their respective team's 20,000. Each manager was then allowed to bid for additional new team members with the remaining points. The provisions of the selection system are carefully spelled out. They cover virtually any situation that might arise when putting teams together. The success of a team is reflected in a manager's ability to select players who, as a group, possess talent, desire to win, and compatible personalities.

To make the system work, we had to have a player agent, someone who would be a combined auctioneer, bookkeeper, and confidant. Once his duties were completed at the beginning of the season, all records were sealed until the selection process the next year.

Our first player agent for Little League was Edwin "Ned" Grove, who stayed with us until 1945, when his work took him out of the area. Since I was no longer managing a team, I took on the job.

Another big plus for the 1940 season was the fact that we had no difficulty finding umpires. Umpiring is a significant service. It can be a decisive force, as it is intended to be, on close plays and in enforcing the rules of the game. We always tried to encourage respect for anyone who exercised this authority for us. We wanted the boys to recognize the umpires as friendly judges on the field and willingly abide by their decisions.

Lundy Lumber took the first-half crown in 1940 with a 6-3 record. Lycoming and Buick each had 5-4 records. Stein's, the new team, won only two games in each half, but those victories proved crucial in determining the final standings in both halves.

Perhaps as a carryover from 1939, Lundy's and Lycoming Dairy became especially keen rivals. One game saw Major Gehron bested by Frank Sipe in a 12-inning pitching duel. Another game was called after eight innings.

When Lycoming won the second half, the championship series became a repeat of the 1939 series. However, this time the competition was more intense. One of the playoff games also ended in a tie.

It was an exciting season for the boys and managers, even when a controversy developed during the final game of the championship series. In the last half of the third inning, Lundy batter Bill Pflegor, a true champion by any standard, stepped up to the plate. He hit a powerful line drive between the left and center fielders. Without an outfield fence, such hits were possible home runs as they bounced on the packed surface created by the large trucks that came and went at the Dean Phipps warehouse just beyond the normal outfield. As Pflegor circled the bases, the first-base umpire looked to see whether he touched each base. Center-fielder Howdy Crossley chased the ball and relayed it to "Tucker" Frazier, who threw to Fred Sander at home plate. Paul Stone, chief umpire, came from his normal position behind the pitcher and gave the "safe" sign as Phlegor's slide beat the throw. It was an exciting play. The Lundy fans cheered wildly.

However, from the player's bench along the third-base line came the excited call to catcher Sander, "Throw it to Dick! He didn't touch third!" As Dick Smith took Saunder's throw, he put his foot on the base and the third-base umpire called the runner out. The excitement among the fans was intense, for the winner of this game would be League Champion.

As I recall, my reaction was twofold. I was pleased that Marty and Harry Forshaw, on the bench with Major Gehron, had known what to do about the missed base. However, the home-plate umpire had called the runner safe, and as head umpire in the game, his decision stood; nevertheless, I was not satisfied with the decision and notified the umpire in chief we were continuing the game under protest.

When the game ended, the score was 3-0, Lundy's. However, since I had registered a protest, the series remained unfinished. In retrospect, I soon realized the protest, while appropriate at the time it was filed, should have been dropped after the game. The missed out had cost Lycoming only one run. Inasmuch as Lundy's had three runs and Lycoming none, that should have been the end of it. My actions were not conducive of a harmonious resolution of the dispute.

As it was, parents of the Lundy team members refused to allow their boys to abide by the decision of the Board of Arbitration a week later when it upheld my protest and ordered the game replayed. With their refusal to play, I found myself in the uncomfortable position of declaring Lycoming Dairy the champion by default. League presidents should not be team managers!

Traumatic though it was at the time, that experience provided a lesson that helped when we wrote the rules for the annual end-of-season tournament that has become known as the Little League World Series. Since then, any such dispute has had to be resolved on the spot by the umpires, from whose decision there is no appeal.

This incident provided lessons which were well learned. We were covering new ground and learning as we went through each unplanned experience. Fortunately, what I was learning would prove to be beneficial to Little League in the future.

Aside from their regular games and practices in 1940, the boys enjoyed the excitement of two very special events we arranged for them. First, they played an exhibition game at the West Branch Fireman's Association annual outing. Being the firemen's picnic guests at Vanrensler Park at Picture Rocks was almost as exciting as their train trip to the New York World's Fair, with all wearing their Little League uniforms.

The uniforms not only provided an easy way for us

to keep track of the boys, but also was a means of recognition for them. I had arranged a schedule for us. At each stop, an announcer welcomed the "Little Leaguers from Williamsport, Pennsylvania" over the public-address system and gave a brief resume of the league's activities. There isn't any doubt that the attention made the boys feel at least a foot taller, but that wasn't the highlight of the fair for them. What they talked about most later was the "Talking Plymouth," a car that had addressed them by name.

When we reviewed our finances after the season ended, we were not in as good financial shape as we had hoped. The New York trip had put us in the red. But, it was worth every penny we spent.

Chapter 8

Fall rains in 1940 did a world of good for our playing field. That made us eager for the third season of Little League baseball almost before the memories of the second season had a chance to settle in.

Generally, we were ready to go when time for the 1941 spring tryouts arrived. Lycoming fielded a fine defensive team. Bobby Tilburg, 9, and Major Gehron, 11, pitched their teammates to eight wins in nine starts to win the first half easily. The three other teams made a tight race of the battle for second place. Lundy's and Stein's threatened throughout the second half, but Lycoming came out on top, taking the championship without a series.

With three championships in a row, Lycoming was beginning to seem fixed in that position. The record shows, however, that it would be six years before Lycoming won the championship again. In the interim, every other team in the league took the title at least once.

Many of the boys were weak at the plate, but several gave opposing pitchers nightmares. Dalton McCloskey, a pitcher for Stein's, demonstrated that not all pitchers are weak hitters. It was his last season of eligibility and he bowed out with an even .500 batting average, the best in the league. Twelve-year-old Al Yearick came in second, at .459. Best of the 11-year-old boys was Bill Witmer, with a .446 average. The difference age and size made was obvious in Jimmy Gehron's .300 average, best among the nine-year-olds.

Not all the honors went to the batters, though.

Lundy's had two strikeout artists on its pitching staff, Allan Meyers and Bud Rich. They both had games during which they fanned 16 batters. That stands as a record in Original Little League.

As in earlier seasons, the league played an exhibition game at mid-season, with its All-Stars competing. That was one of the ways we continued to introduce Little League to the rest of the community.

As for the players, the most exciting game of the season was probably one between the New York Yankees and the Philadelphia Athletics at Shibe Park in Philadelphia. We took all of the boys, in uniform, down by train. Like the adults with them, the Little Leaguers were eager to see whether Joe Dimaggio would continue his hitting streak. He did, before 40,000 fans.

We toured Independence Hall and other historical sites around the city. But again, it was the little things that had the biggest effect. The boys were particularly excited about putting coins in the slots to unlock the doors to food at an automat.

Just as at the World's Fair in New York, the boys in their uniforms aroused curiosity and interest in Little League baseball.

Though we had cut our budget deficit in half and had a wonderful season, we had little time to enjoy it, for the league was given notice by the owner of the field site that we would have to vacate at the end of the summer. Lycoming Motors, later known as Avco Lycoming, needed the site to build an addition to its plant for stepped-up production of military-aircraft engines.

Later in the season, I had to find a new manager for the Buick team. Once again I turned to Howard Gair for guidance. Following his advice, I recruited Martin L.

"Marty" Miller. Marty was dedicated to Little League and served 18 consecutive years, managing more Original Little League games than any other man.

Contributions like Marty's can't be measured by the number of championships won, although four of his teams came out on top. It's by what they have meant to individual boys that they are measured. Marty followed his boys proudly as they competed in high school and college, and beyond as they made their own contributions to society.

Marty's selfless labors for Little League included some pretty memorable moments, like the time he acted as an impromptu steel-rigger 20 feet in the air on 600-pound bleacher sections while volunteers on the ground balanced them. He was there to lend a hand at 1:30 on a cold and snowy January morning when we unloaded a truckload of seat planks. And he was there to paint fences by lantern light after games. Self-giving like Marty's undergirded everything that brought Little League to national and world recognition and acceptance.

As we scurried around looking for a new site, we made an encouraging discovery. The completion of a flood-control dike along Lycoming Creek in Max M. Brown Memorial Park made that spot more suitable than ever. Although city council had denied permission to build a field there in 1939, I was not convinced the decision couldn't be reversed.

The generally flat plot I had in mind lay about six feet below West Fourth Street, the city's main east-west highway. It was nestled between the street and the 20-foot-high dike to the south.

The site was more spacious and more desirable than the one we were being forced to vacate. Beautiful tall trees outside the probable playing area provided a natural attraction we couldn't have matched anywhere. There were 10 stately maples scattered about the western section and three American Elms in the east. Gracious elms were equally spaced along the street and a great old Lombardy poplar stood sentinel-like on the bank, about 30 feet behind the spot where home plate would be.

George, Johnny, Marty, Mac, and I met one Sunday to look over the site and consider its possibilities. We were all impressed. I think we all believed our chances of success were good this time. Things were different now. In 1939, we were just trying to create a league. Now, we were getting ready to begin our fourth season. Then, no one had heard of Little League. As a matter of fact, we didn't even have a name then. Now, everyone in Williamsport who cared about boys or baseball had heard of Little League. Then, I was trying to persuade an old administration. Now, a new administration occupied city hall.

The new council liked my proposal and gave the league its approval. The only obstacle might be the U.S. Army Corps of Engineers. Since the corps of engineers had constructed the dike, and its jurisdiction extended beyond the base of it onto the proposed playing area, I had to obtain the corps' approval before we could proceed.

I was graciously received by the Corps' resident engineer, E.J. Luetje. He was in charge of the dike project on both sides of the Susquehanna River and along Lycoming Creek. After I explained our dilemma, the need for a new field, he gave me the approval I needed. The only stipulation was continued Army Corps access to the area. Things were moving ahead.

When I returned to city council with the corps' approval and our plans for laying out the field, I thought we had things pretty well worked out. I presented my field design. We had planned to cut down one small tree about 2-½-inches in diameter so we could orient the field to minimize the effect of the glare caused by the setting sun. Our games are always played in the evenings, I explained. The council was adamant: the tree must stay! The tree remained, five feet beyond the first-base coach's box.

The need to change the field brought me into a new and closer relationship with Mac McCloskey. All of us adults involved in Little League were aware of Mac's contribution the past year as our ever-faithful scorekeeper. Now he threw himself into helping us prepare for the 1942 season. He dismantled the bleachers at the old field and hauled them to his garage for storage until we had a place prepared for them at the new field, which we began building that spring.

The exactness with which Mac worked as a tool designer at Lycoming Motors made him the ideal person to lay out the field. With that done, we stripped the sod three feet wide down the first-and third-base lines and in circles around home plate and the pitcher's mound. That went fairly quickly, but stripping the arc for infielders' play kept us busy for several nights after we dismissed the boys from tryout sessions.

At last, we got to the backstop and bleachers Mac had stored in his garage. He even donated players' benches. He was a dynamo of ideas as he skillfully worked with the other managers to plan and build fences, dugouts, a club-house, and more bleachers. His scale model of a concession stand was the design we used later when we built a real one. His detailed scale drawings of the playing field became the blueprint from which hundreds of Little League fields would be build all over America.

With the 1942 tryouts and player auction out of the

way, I began looking for ways to bring our boys recognition in the community. I had them march in the annual Memorial Day parade.

Heading our contingent were two unsuccessful player candidates wearing rented costumes. One was dressed as a cowboy and one as a drum major. They carried a large cutout eagle between them. I had lettered "Little League" on its outstretched wings.

When I read the congratulatory comments in the papers the next day, they referred to our boys as the "Little Eagles." I began to think that we needed a more-baseball-oriented emblem to identify the league, so I got busy and designed a baseball diamond and a waving flag inside a keystone, to represent Pennsylvania as the state where Little League was founded. A slightly modified version of that design has been used ever since by Little League.

When the season opened, we noticed that more and more adults were coming out to watch the boys play. Perhaps it was the new field that was attracting attention. Or perhaps it was the increasing press coverage we were receiving. There were bigger headlines and longer commentaries about our activities. Whatever the reason, we were happy about it.

It was a tight race among well-balanced teams, but thanks to the excellent pitching of Bill Newcomer, Stein's finished the first half in first place. The boys' play was steadily improving and sportswriters were commenting about it.

As the hotly contested second round moved toward the end of our most exciting season yet, fans turned out in greater and greater numbers. When from 500 to 600 fans began showing up from all over the city, we were forced to build more stands and replace missing parts on stands the city made available to us.

Stein's seemed headed unchallenged toward the league championship, with 17 victories and only three defeats. However, George Bebble's choice of Ed Yonkin to pitch the last game of the season against Stein's changed the picture. Ed not only pitched Lundy's to victory, but he did it with the first no-hit, no-run game in Little League's four-year history. That tied Lundy's with Stein's and forced a second-half playoff. Lundy's took it when Whitey Johnson made his team's only hit, in the last inning.

In the championship series, with Lundy leading by two games to one, the teams played to a 1-1 tie in the fourth game. But Lundy's, not to be denied, exploded with hits in the fifth game, clinching the title with an 11-5 victory. Lundy's showed that with small boys as well as with major-leaguers, a hot streak at the right time can take a team all the way to the championship.

That year left us with great memories of the players. Some of the language we used, though simple and obvious to us, was not always clear to the younger boys. When we read off the names of those who didn't make the teams for 1942 and announced they were on "reserve teams," little Ted Slopey didn't hear it quite that way.

Moving close to me and looking straight into my face, he said, "Gee, Tuck, I sure am glad I made the reverse team."

Reserve or reverse, morning or minor league, the name really made no difference to him and many other boys. They were simply overjoyed at having the opportunity to play regularly. After 1942, they, too, played in uniform.

The three youngest boys on each Little League team also played in the Morning League. In one league, they sat on the bench most of the time hoping to be called as substitutes. In the other league, they were the stars. They were the tie that bound the leagues together.

During the 1942-43 off-season, some of us among the managing personnel built 270 feet of portable wooden fence. In the spring, we erected it around the outfield, from foul line to foul line. The boys had yearned for the day when they would have a wall to challenge their hitting powers. Before we went to work, though, I had to untangle some red tape to get permission to proceed.

My visit to the Department of Parks ended in disappointment. The response was that our request, if granted, would violate the conditions under which the city had accepted the land as a memorial to Max M. Brown. At face value, that meant the fence was out of the question.

Not content to be turned down as a result of a city official's negative interpretation of a legal document, I went to the county court house to check the deed for myself. To my pleasant surprise, I found a clause stipulating that a marker should be erected designating the site as the Max M. Brown Memorial Park. The city had failed to do that.

With this knowledge in hand, I paid another visit to city hall. After explaining the results of my research, I expressed the willingness of Little League to include a panel on the proposed fence large enough to contain the Max M. Brown Memorial Park designation. We'd balance the panel aesthetically with one of like size and paint a scoreboard on it. The rest of the fence, I explained, would be in sections. We planned to build it so that any section could be temporarily removed to provide easy access to the field, if necessary.

This time I left city hall with the permission we needed.

It didn't take George, Johnny, Marty, Mac, and me long to construct the prefabricated fence. I borrowed a truck from my boss and we hauled the sections to the field. The fence's portability, of which we were so proud, had an undesirable aspect we weren't aware of until circumstances revealed it dramatically a few years later. But, at the time we installed it, the fence served the purpose we had intended. It added a new element of excitement to the game. The stronger batters now could know the thrill of hitting a ball over the fence and out of the park for an automatic home run. The fence completed the process of defining the size of the playing field.

The "home run" fence was the first of a rapid sequence of additions and innovations in 1943 and 1944 at our permanent location. Enthusiasm to see that our boys had the best facilities possible was spreading like pennant fever near the end of a hard-fought season. It seemed everybody wanted to contribute to the improvements. Little League was still pretty much our own four teams and the reserve teams, but it was developing an imagination-stretching image. Each step forward gave future Little Leagues something more to strive for in their field facilities.

Chapter 9

Little League's fifth season began with 137 boys trying out. We couldn't accommodate all of them, but we made a valiant effort. With four major-league and four minor-league teams, we had more than 100 boys in uniform that year.

Our Little Leaguers were newly outfitted. We handed down their old uniforms to the Morning League. The new uniforms not only had the team name on the shirt front, but also carried large numerals on the back.

Another innovation that year was the new league-provided schedules. Printed on lightweight cardboard in a twofold arrangement to fit the pocket, they contained game dates and a rundown on each player, manager, sponsor, and contributor. Eventually, we were able to incorporate cumulative records of championship teams, batting champions, and no-hit, no-run pitchers. The original pencil drawing is still used today.

Another first in 1943 was that my office schedule became a factor in my on-field involvement with the league. My employer had scheduled me to work regular daytime hours one week and from 11 a.m. to early evening the next. That meant I had to find a new manager for Lycoming Dairy.

Bill Bair, the league's 1939 batting champion, was ready and able to move in. In 1940, he had supervised the reserve players in their morning games. He had also played in the West End League for teenagers. When exploring the possibility, in 1941-42, of older boys taking an active part in the program, I'd had him working with me as an assistant manager. Bill handled the responsibilities well, with his team narrowly losing the second-half crown and a chance at the championship.

My freedom to move about during the mornings in alternate weeks turned into an advantage for the league. It enabled me to continue coming up with the supplies I needed to build sideline fences and improve the general appearance of the field.

Howard Gair was now our official head umpire. His son, Vance, a willing volunteer, had umpired 21 games before he left for the navy in midseason of 1942. As the league became more established and more parents became involved, umpires became easier to recruit. Frank Rizzzo umpired 20 games in 1943, when his son wasn't playing. In 1944, he handled 43 games; a year later, 44. When George Bebble received his "Greetings From the President," Frank moved from umpire to manager of the Lundy team. When Lincoln Little League was formed in 1946, he again volunteered his services. He and many others dedicated themselves to Little League to make it a great success for the boys in spite of the difficult times.

In August, we unveiled our "Armed Services Honor Roll" listing the names of our Little League volunteers who had been called into the armed services. The V.F.W. donated an American flag to be flown from the 20-foot steel pole we had erected in center field. This was our way of keeping the boys aware of the sacrifice men they knew were making for our country.

Attendance at the games that season continued to increase and so did the contributions. We were averaging $5.69 per game. When we sought personal assistance from businessmen and city, county, and state officials to pay for the "home-run fence," they put $47 in the league treasury. At midseason, Lundy Lumber Company, as eager as we to see improvements made rapidly, spurred us on by paying 1944 and 1945 sponsorship fees in advance. Meanwhile, Mac and the Williamsport Recreation Commission each donated a dozen balls. The Parks Department tossed in a set of bases.

At season's end, we were finally out of the red and had some breathing space, for the uniforms did not have to be replaced for another year. Things were looking up.

The pennant race was almost a carbon copy of 1942, with Stein's winning both halves, eliminating the need for a championship series.

As a result of the fine seasonal play, the fans clamored for more, so we picked two all-star teams from Lundy's, Lycoming, and Buick and named them the Stars and the Stripes. The Stripes won the opportunity to play the league champions — and took that series, too! The most unusual game of that series was a no-hitter by Stein's Chuck Cogley, which the Stripes won, 2-0. Stein's had only one ineffective hit.

At the annual banquet, I was impressed all over again with the small stature of the Little Leaguers. In dress clothes, they reminded me that they were small boys who liked to play baseball, not baseball players who just happened to be small boys. That helped me keep things in proper perspective.

At the banquet, we paid tribute to 12-year-old Tom Sweeley, the batter with the second-highest average. Tom was waging a courageous battle against rheumatic fever. Every player in the league signed a letter to him which I delivered later in the evening along with a medal recognizing his batting prowess. Little Leaguers were there for one another, time and time again.

At Christmas time, continuing a practice begun in 1942, each manager sent a greeting card with the team picture on it to each of his players and to the other managers.

Special events kept Little League continually exciting for the boys. We constantly provided "big" things for them to do. But, our major emphasis was the field itself. The game was for the boys, but the fun was for all of us, league personnel included as we planned and worked to improve playing conditions. Our joy was in the doing and in the pleasure the changes brought the boys, and in the fact that "outsiders," persons not officially involved, kept offering helpful services of their own.

Jacob Lehn was one such person. His son was a pitcher-infielder on the Lycoming team. Mr. Lehn built a portable electric scoreboard for us. Storing it at the field in the room beneath the rest rooms, he would install it on top of the fence at game time. He sat behind it on a stool to operate the knife switches to indicate balls, strikes, and outs.

I was also able to salvage several hundred feet of exterior electrical wiring. With the Department of Parks' permission, we strung the wire from the rest room service box through the trees along Fourth Street even though we had no need for it, yet. Bob Stout, a Williamsport Technical Institute student living in the neighborhood, soon put it to use.

As part of his work in a course on radio communication, Bob had built an amplifier. He volunteered to bring his amplifier to the field to announce the lineups before the games and the names of the players as they came to bat. At each game, he set up his equipment behind the fence along the third-base line. Through Bob, Little League was providing an additional thrill every time a boy stepped up to the plate.

Before the 1943 season ended, Bob joined the Merchant Marines. Knowing how much his public-address system meant to the boys, he offered to sell it to us at a reasonable price, and we bought it. Within a short time, Mac McCloskey added a record turntable and a number of records to our equipment inventory. He also took over as announcer.

With Mac in charge, the games began promptly on time. The ritual began with the announcement of the team lineups, followed by the playing of the national anthem. Between innings and half-innings, he played John Philip Sousa marches. The games were never official until he gave the summary and played Kate Smith's rendition of "God Bless America." Through Mac's electronics, the "band" Major and Jimmy had asked me about five years earlier, now "showed up" at every game. Unfortunately, Major was no longer one of the players. His eligibility had ended with the 1942 season.

Postgame time, too, quickly became a ritual for many Little Leaguers and their fans. Mac would play marches while he prepared the box score for the newspapers. Many of the older folks stayed to listen and to talk to the players, praising their play and offering encouragement. The boys' fine play, the special features we added, and Mac's performance drew more and more people to the games.

"I was never a baseball fan," said one regular, "but this is something I really enjoy. I'm here for every game."

His comments were echoed by others.

One of the regulars, George Stecher, who later

became an umpire, let us know that some of the fans couldn't read the numbers on the scoreboard. With larger crowds, many were too far away or off to the side to see well. George came up with a set of 9x9-inch sheet-metal squares on which he had painted a green background and large, white numbers. We painted a large scoreboard on a new, solid section of the Home Run fence, and Jacob Lehn mounted his electric colored-light balls-strikes-outs board on it.

We had set out to make our field the best in Pennsylvania. With the help of one unanticipated volunteer after another, we were improving the facilities more rapidly than any of us would have thought possible in 1939. Carefully supervised baseball for small boys certainly had a way of bringing out the best in people.

Our highly successful 1943 season pointed to an even better one in 1944. Enthusiasm was running high. Managing personnel were more eager than ever to add to and improve facilities at the field. More boys than ever wanted to try out for the teams. Fan interest continued to grow.

Long before the on-field work for 1944 was upon us, we planned much of what we hoped to do. First item on our agenda was to construct a storage building for working tools, playing equipment, and a press box with a place where Mac could keep score. Part of the 10-foot side facing the diamond was hinged to swing inward and provide Mac with an eight-foot-long desk. We had city council's permission to build provided we dismantled the structure at the end of the season. The 6x10-foot prefabricated building we designed was soon referred to as the clubhouse.

By July, the continuing increase in attendance at

games challenged us to provide more seating facilities. It was too late in the season to build more seats for 1944, but we set to work immediately preparing for 1945.

We planned to build two new bleacher sections with seating capacity for 252 fans. Confair Warehouse, where I worked, would be our workshop. By October 20, we had poured the bleacher foundation and purchased our supplies.

We were nearly ready for the 1945 season opener when excavating was begun for Lycoming Motors' plant expansion. Mac, who was employed there, promptly arranged to get the fill we needed to raise right field to the level of the rest of the field. Clair Bishop, plant manager, not only granted Mac's request for fill, but also allowed him to use company equipment to haul and spread it. His only stipulation was that Norm Phillips, the equipment operator, must do the hauling on Sunday. Norm readily agreed and we soon had the fill.

Norm refused Mac's offer to pay for his services, so Mac came up with a gift of appreciation. With the war on, cigarettes were limited to one pack per purchase. Ever resourceful, Mac enlisted the help of others to accumulate the 10 packs needed for a full carton. To sweeten Norm's gift more, he added a 12-pack of soft drinks.

After Norm rough-graded the fill, we brought in topsoil, raked it, and sowed grass seed. The timing was just right, for the new grass was ready when the 1945 season opened.

One of the most valuable improvements for 1945 was strictly Mac's doing. He worked all winter engineering and building a remote-control system for electronically recording balls, strikes, and outs instantaneously from the press box. With a flip of the switch, he could flash the umpire's call with red or green lights on the outfield scoreboard. Typically, Mac built both scoreboard and control box at his own expense. Other members of our volunteer group dug the trench and laid the conduit from the press-box control to the scoreboard.

That spring we obtained the additional topsoil we needed and put up an eight-foot-high wire screen along each sideline to protect bleacher fans from foul balls.

Most important of all, however, were the "Home" and "Visiting" team dugouts we built. It seemed to us these "private" places for managers and players were long over-due. Heretofore, any consultation with the players or guidance by the managers had to be in full sight of the fans and opposing players. Dugouts would enable managers to point out mistakes and offer direction without risk of embarrassing their boys before the crowd.

So that fans in the bleachers behind them would have an unobstructed view of the game, we designed the dugouts to be partly below field level. For the first time, we hired construction workers — to build the forms, install the drains, and pour concrete floors. We volunteers worked into the night after tryouts to complete the dugout walls, roof, and seats.

By the opening game of the 1945 season, the boys has as nearly a "big league" park and facilities as we could envision. It had taken us more than six seasons to accomplish it, and we were proud of what we had done.

People were recognizing the value of Little League and what I had intended for the program. The night I was to attend a Newberry Lions Club testimonial dinner in my honor, I was flattered by an article in a local paper. It credited the interest generated by Little League for inspiring the formation of leagues for boys over 12.

At the dinner, I made sure all knew how much I appreciated the men who worked so closely with me to make Little League successful. I couldn't help remembering all the times my dad had taken me to big-league games when I was a boy. The fact that he was there to share the honor with me made it all the sweeter. The highlight of the evening, though, was Mayor Leo Williamson's delivery of a telegram from Maryville, Tennessee, sent to me in care of city hall. It read:

> UNCLE TUCK SORRY CANNOT BE WITH YOU TONIGHT
>
> GRATEFULLY YOURS.
>
> MAJOR AND JIM GEHRON

I was happy that, in spirit, at least, they were sharing this joyous occasion with me.

The following evening, the Sun editorialized that Little League was the "best antidote for juvenile delinquency." It said Little League was attracting the attention of visitors to the city and was being copied elsewhere. The publicity we were receiving through the newspapers was spreading the word about the benefits of our program.

Why all the special attention during the spring of 1944? I believe the reason was my impending call to service in the navy. In fact, it was mentioned to me during the dinner. The word soon got around, leaving people who knew me a little surprised when they continued to run into me on the street. There was no mystery. Soon after the night of the dinner, the government revised draft regulations to exempt men of my age group from service. I had gotten as far as the reception center at New Cumberland, near Harrisburg, before being turned back.

The Newberry Lions Club hadn't climbed on the bandwagon when it became involved in Little League; it had helped build it. In 1947, it provided medals for players in Little League's first national tournament. The Community Trade Association, forerunner of the Greater Williamsport Chamber of Commerce, had been invited to sponsor the medals that would carry the name "Williamsport, Pa." into communities around the nation. The C.T.A. saved $14 by passing up the opportunity.

Little League's sixth season brought in two new managers. Ollie Fawcett, who had been unable to accept an invitation to manage in 1939, took over the Lycoming Dairy team. Bill Falk became manager of Lundy Lumber, succeeding Frank Rizzo.

Ollie's predecessor, Bill Bair, the teenage manager, had done well with Lycoming in 1943 but had run into irreconcilable scheduling difficulties. Games of the Central League team on which he played and of the Little League team he managed frequently fell on the same evenings. The only way he saw to resolve the conflict so he could continue to play was to quit managing. Assurance that he had made the right decision came a few years later when he was named a varsity pitcher for Penn State University.

Bill Falk did an admirable job of rebuilding Lundy's to a competitive position during his three years with the team. Ollie, it turned out, was embarking on a period of service to children that would continue well over four decades. In his first year, his team dealt Buick its only defeat of the regular season.

In the years since, Ollie's teams have won five championships, including one string of three in succession. Five of his boys became league batting champions;

nine others took batting honors in their age groups. One of Ollie's special contributions has been in coaching his pitchers to take advantage of their teammates' fielding abilities. The result has been that five of the league's nine not-hit, no-run games in 43 seasons were pitched by boys on Ollie's team.

In 1965, the Fawcetts moved across the mountain from Williamsport. Despite the long drive, Ollie showed up regularly on his team's game nights. During those years, Ollie and his wife, Helen, never used distance as an excuse to avoid participating in league activities. In fact, one year Helen joined my wife, Grayce, in going far beyond the call of duty to paint the outfield fence. After a number of years, the Fawcetts moved back to the city.

Ollie, quiet and unassuming, is a living testimonial that a nice guy can finish first. The esteem of the many youngsters who have played baseball under his tutelage is convincing testimony.

Spring was just 10 days old when I invited all candidates for the 1944 Little League and their parents to watch the American League's movie of the 1943 World Series. I used the occasion to announce the first preseason practice.

When we completed the tryouts and player auction, the Sun ran a lengthy article explaining how the auction system worked. It followed up with "a series of four articles on the prospects of the various teams in the Little League for the 1944 season." Each article was written by an official Little League volunteer. Sportswriters and fans throughout the city were taking Little League seriously because the league's adult volunteers took themselves seriously.

In 1944, it quickly became obvious that Buick had

an unusually talented team compared to the rest of the league. Their only loss was to Lycoming Dairy, by a single run. But what an exciting time the boys had competing in that 5-4 battle. The presence of Connie Mack, the 81-year-old owner-manager of the Philadelphia Athletics, and the largest crowd ever to witness a regular league game made it a special occasion. The Grand Old Man of Baseball, as he was popularly known, had his A's in town to play an exhibition game with the Williamsport Grays. Like so many others, Mr. Mack was much impressed with the boys' performance.

That season the Little Leaguers again played an exhibition game in Bowman Field before an overflow crowd. The game pitted teams of 12-year-olds, boys in their last season of eligibility, against each other. Such appearances continued to expose small boys' baseball to people beyond the city.

Although Little Leaguers had executed numerous double plays during the first five seasons, the triple play had continued to elude them. The sixth season was to be the year of the triple play, two of them. Both were made within a five-day period — by losing teams!

Look-alike nine-year-old twins, Ed and Jim Senate, who began their careers that season with Lycoming Dairy, quickly became crowd pleasers. Because of their extremely small size, they soon ran into a problem. All the small bats on the Lycoming team had been broken. The two boys, just 49-½-inches tall and together weighing just about 100 pounds, had to use the heavier, longer bats. They used to alternate on the Lycoming team, sharing the same uniform, prompting a local reporter to write that although the Lycoming team was to play at Memorial Park, he couldn't be sure which of the twins would play. It was impossible to tell them apart.

In 1945, the two became battery mates for Lycoming, with Ed pitching and Jim catching, and each wore a new uniform. They made league history in 1947 as 12-year-olds. That season Jim, posting a .473 average, led the league in batting. Ed became the third Little Leaguer to pitch a no-hit, no-run game, just weeks after Jim Hart had become the first 11-year-old Little Leaguer to accomplish that feat.

When the league completed its schedule in 1944, there was no championship series. Buick had made that unnecessary with its superior performance throughout the season. To satisfy fan demand for more games, we named an all-star team from the other three teams in the league to meet Buick in postseason play. First, though, to entertain the boys and give the All-Stars opportunity to play together before their important five-game series, the adult volunteers challenged them to a game.

Not certain what to call them, the press referred to the adult team as the Graybeards, Old Timers, Misfits, and Has Beens. The latter designation appeared in their part of the box score in the newspaper after the All-Stars drubbed them, 14-6, a result due in part to the volunteers' sloppy fielding.

Along with the fun, the game between the boys and their leaders had a serious purpose. Contributions from fans, who turned out in good numbers for the contest, went into a players' fund from which boys in need could borrow to buy gloves. We allowed them to repay the loans by doing specified small chores at the field. We continued the games and the fund every year thereafter.

The All-Stars' performance in the series gave Buick all it could handle, playing to a 9-9 tie in the first game and splitting the next four games. Buick, however, was not be denied. In the deciding sixth game, it put the exclamation point on its championship. After Buick's two-run homer in the first was matched by an All-Stars' two-run homer in the second, Buick closed the door and went on to win the game, 5-2.

The usual banquet closed out the 1944 season, which had seen hard-hitting 12-year old Mark Lindemuth take the league batting championship with a spectacular .565 average. He'd had 26 hits in 46 at-bats. Four of his hits had been home runs, also a record for the season.

As in 1944, we ended the season in the black. For the first time, though, the biggest source of income was game-time contributions from the fans. With new uniforms unnecessary until 1946 and a nice balance in the league treasury, we felt confident about moving ahead with further improvements of field and facilities.

More and more boys wanted to play in Little League. Spring of 1945 saw 150 turn out for the first practice. We had to turn more than 20 away because they lived outside the league boundary. I told the newspaper I'd like to see another league formed in the east end of the city.

That April 20, we showed the boys and their parents a movie of the 1944 Major League World Series. In those pre-TV days, such showings were big events.

The season was highlighted by an invitation from the Kiwanis Club to join the Williamsport Grays as guests at a luncheon meeting at the city's best-known hotel, the Lycoming. The boys showed up in full uniform and joined in the applause as I accepted the Kiwanis merit pin in recognition of my part in Little League.

Continuing good newspaper coverage, no doubt, was the reason for the continuing steady increase in attendance at games. By the time the playoffs ended, an estimated 15,000, including many regulars, had proved the value of the new seating facilities.

So appealing had the championship series become that we had 2,000 programs printed. We could have used more. Bill Kehoe of the *Grit* noted that the Little League playoffs were attracting more attention than the Williamsport Grays.

The first-half tie between Buick and Stein's was broken in a three-game series won by Buick. In the second half, both teams came to the last game in a dead heat. This time, though, Stein's came out ahead. After trailing three games to one in the seven-game series, Johnny Lindemuth left for his annual family vacation, and I had the good fortune of substituting for him as his Stein's team won the next three games and became the league champion.

Chapter 10

With the war over, America entered a new era. A sense of freedom and destiny permeated the nation, including the boys and adults in Little League.

Adults from other sections of the city and from other communities came to us asking how they could form leagues like ours. We were thrilled to be sought out and did our best to share whatever information we thought would be of value to them.

Anticipating another outstanding year for Little League, we ordered new uniforms early in February 1946. We purchased lumber to extend the left- and right-field sideline fences to meet the home-run fence and ordered denim cloth and filler so Grayce and Helen could work at their leisure to make 100 bleacher cushions.

Just as winter was bowing out on the calendar, we bought lumber to build 32 lineal feet of eight-row elevated bleachers to install behind the first-base dugout. They would add another 192 to our seating capacity.

Everything was moving smoothly toward the playing season. The tryouts had gone well, the player auction was behind us, and the team squads were being molded into effective playing units. The uniforms were expected to arrive any day, and the bleacher parts were ready to be moved to the field for final assembly. A $110 contribution from the Williamsport Wheel Club added to our sense of well-being.

Our situation was ideal. It seemed nothing could impede our progress. We had no way of knowing Mother Nature would challenge us to action beyond our wildest imagination — or worst fears — to delay our season's opening. She would make 1946 both different and memorable for Little League's players and managing personnel.

"RIVER RISES TOWARD HIGH-WATER MARK"screamed a newspaper headline, May 27. Williamsport awaited the first big test of the dikes that had been built after the devastating 1936 flood.

The crest of the flood arrived at 3:30 a.m., May 31. That day two big headlines told the story:"RAGING LYCOMING SWEPT FOLLOWING CLOUDBURST"and"30-FOOT FLOOD HITS WEST BRANCH."

My home was on high ground about half a mile upstream from the Little League field and two blocks from the creek. Properties nearer the creek, like Confair Bottling Company, my employer, were threatened. If the wild stream went out of control and the dikes could not contain it, a severly damaging flood would result. I moved about constantly all morning inspecting the plant and warehouses, trying to anticipate possible danger points in the area. The main threat appeared to be from underground water pressure; I feared it would cause the concrete floor of the plant's basement boiler room to buckle. We were prepared to drill a few holes to relieve the pressure, but decided to wait after tests indicated that waiting was the better course.

The creek is 250 feet from the Confair plant. As we monitored the water level, we breathed easier, for it was gradually receding. Workers who hadn't already gone to homes that were endangered were relieved of their duties so they could assist friends whose homes were in threatened or flooded areas of the city.

It was then that I thought of Little League. Notwithstanding the fact that the field was on the other side of the creek and should be protected by the dike just beyond the home-run fence, I thought I'd better take a look.

Walking to the field was easy. I simply crossed the nearby Memorial Avenue Bridge, then walked about half a mile on the dike. At that point, I stood above center field looking over a lake where Little League Field should have been. In the distance, the tops of the backstop posts were the only identifying features I could see. Later, we determined that the water had been almost 11 feet deep at the backstop. It had covered the press box as well as West Fourth Street 20 feet beyond.

As I walked back to Confair's, I saw a section of the Little League bleachers floating near the grandstand entrance to Bowman Field, more than 360 yards as the crow flies from where the rising water had lifted it from its foundation. There was nothing I could do about it, so I kept on walking.

Conditions at Confair's were still improving, so I went on home, where Grayce and the girls were eagerly waiting for me to take them on a tour of the flood sites. After we crossed the creek on the High Street Bridge, we circled about from one high-level street to another until we arrived at the intersection of West Fourth, Beeber, and Oliver Streets, near the northeast corner of Little League Field. The Fawcetts had arrived there just ahead of us. Ollie and his teenage daughter, Helen Louise, and her friend Mary Ellen Boyer, were already in the water rescuing one of the floating bleacher sections.

When the dike was built along Lycoming Creek, an opening around the railroad bridge about a quarter of a mile downstream from Memorial Park had never been closed. Before that could be done, the bridge and the roadbed for the railroad had to be raised. It was this opening that allowed the water to back into the park.

When the water reached the Little League bleachers, it raised the slotted main supports off the concrete piers. The first section dislodged and went with the westward flow to Bowman Field. The other, perhaps held captive by a nearby tree, apparently didn't leave its mooring until the water began receding. Then the reversed flow carried it eastward about 200 feet, where it lodged against some trees.

Leaving Monya Lee and Karen with Grayce, I waded into the water and helped Ollie, Helen Louise, and Mary Ellen push the floating stand to a tree within six feet of its proper location. Then we tied it fast so that, as the water receded, we could align it with the highest pier. That done, the front of the section slowly settled into alignment with the lower pier supports as the water level fell, saving us the laborious chore of dismantling and reassembling it.

About the time we completed our rescue of the bleacher section, Mac appeared. He, Ollie, and I decided that if we didn't get the section at Bowman Field back while it was afloat, we'd have to take it apart and return it piece by piece. The Bowman Field side of Memorial Park is about as low as the Little League Field, so we knew the water would be quite deep. Wading it was out of the question.

Mac finally hit on the idea that we thought might work. His son, Dalton, and a friend, Danny Free, had been building a kayak. Although it wasn't finished, it might float. It was worth checking out, we decided.

Mac and I walked the four blocks to his home and carried the kayak back. Then, I waded west about 100 yards in three-foot-deep water on West Fourth Street, pushing the kayak beside me. At that point, I had to leave the highway, venturing into water 10 feet deep for the next 100 yards north of the street. Being a nonswimmer, I got into the kayak and tested it before leaving the highway.

Finding no leaks, I began paddling cautiously toward the floating bleachers. The adventure was more frightening than thrilling.

When I finally made it to the bleachers, I crawled aboard and carefully pulled the kayak after me. I had no choice but to sit on the angled edge of a 2x10-inch seat plank. Having found the most secure and comfortable position I could, I began to paddle. I was able to steer a course that took my 16x16-foot "raft" through the picnic grove and around the cookhouse and pavilion. I was afraid the section might not clear the comparatively shallow water over the street, but everything was working to our advantage. Once I got through the grove, I was able to set a straight course to the bleachers already tethered to a tree.

Ollie and Mac awaited my arrival and tied the bleachers to another tree. The only uncertainty now was whether the water level would drop rapidly enough for us to hook the top of the section to the piers before dark. We managed to make the alignment with the piers at the top of the bank, but it was many hours later before the bleachers could settle completely into place. Fortunately, the flood crested on a Friday, so we were free over the weekend and able to guide the bleachers onto their foundation without a hitch as the water slowly drained away.

The Little League part of Memorial Park is a small basin. After the water receded to the level of the opening at the railroad bridge where it came in, the rest of the water had nowhere to go except into the air or into the ground until the creek level dropped enough to allow a small nearby stream to drain it off.

What seemed so long, then, was really less than a week, so on the seventh day after the high-water mark, we were back in business. That day, June 6, the newspaper reported that we had cleared the flood debris from the playing field and Buick and Lycoming would work out that evening. Next night, Lundy's and Hemperly's, first-year successor to Stein's, would take the field.

Of course, the fact that the boys were able to practice did not mean that everything had been restored to preflood condition. For example, 14 sections of the Home Run fence had been lifted off their steel posts and washed away. Some were still unaccounted for 10 days later. Except for Mac, the managing personnel worked long and hard at putting the fence back and otherwise getting the field in top shape again. Mac, as the *Sun* reported, was "busily occupied" with the electrical equipment, public-address system, record player, electric scoreboard, and remote-control scoring panel, all of which were sub-merged in the flood waters.

Once we had the emergency cleanup and repairs taken care of, we moved on to the improvements we had planned over the winter. We intended to double the seating capacity with new bleachers, and extend the sideline fences, completely enclosing the field. We also planned to build a retaining wall and a paved terrace to accommodate league officials and special guests. We decided we could postpone the planned repainting of all structures until later. At any rate, we had more than enough projects lined up to keep us from getting bored.

The record shows the boys helped clean up the field after the flood. Thanks to their help, Lycoming Dairy and Lundy Lumber squared off June 18, starting the season just two weeks behind schedule.

Each season, it seemed, one or more of the boys would do something that hadn't been done before in our league. As in the majors, there were always records to be set and records to be surpassed. Doing something uniquely different put Tom Seewald's name in headlines. When the season was only a few days old, he smacked a home run over the dike. That was undoubtedly the longest home run in the eight years of Little League play. It mattered little that his team, Buick, scored only that one run and lost to Lundy's, 12-1. Tom's powerful blast was a league record and the major topic of conversation that evening.

Lundy's victory, of course, was no fluke. Bill Falk, in his third and last year as manager, had put together a good team. With a 6-3 won-lost record, his boys took the first-half title.

During the second half, another youngster showed Lundy's some exciting home-run power. The headlines declared: "Baidy Smacks Two As Mates Win 10-3."

What was really unusual, Hemperly's third baseman, Francis Baidy, hit both homers in the same inning, part of a second-inning assault that left Lundy's with a 9 0 deficit from which it never recovered. Lundy's lost, 10-3.

In the playoffs for the league championship, Buick, the second-half winner, took the best-of-seven series, 4-1-1.

After the series was tied at one victory each, the boys played to a 10-10 tie, the game being called at the end of the sixth inning because of darkness. After the game, the sponsor of the Buick team went into the dugout and unwittingly broke a league rule. As reported to me by Buick manager Marty Miller, Tommy Richardson sought to spur Marty's boys to victory by promising them a trip to Philadelphia to see the Athletics play, if they won the championship series.

Realizing the promise had probably been made on the spur of the moment with no intent to interfere with league policy, I saw no point in making an issue of it.

Instead, I immediately advised the managers that no matter which team won, all players would go to Philadelphia. It was the most diplomatic way I knew to maintain the policy that sponsors provided financial support but had no voice in running the team that bore their name. It also upheld the policy that no special inducements could be offered one team as a reward for victory over another. The managers and I were eager to keep things that way.

During a break in the series schedule that year, Little League introduced Morning League, our farm system, to the public in an evening game. Twenty-four youngsters showed their talents as the Red Sox eked out a 7-6 victory over the Tigers.

As the year 1946 ended, the *Sun* ran a three-column headline in mammoth type proudly proclaiming:

GROWTH OF SANDLOT BASEBALL GREAT HERE

Response to the accompanying article, regarding the explosion of sports interest in the first postwar year, was euphoric. Attendance at games throughout the Eastern league, which operated out of Williamsport, had topped a million.

Baseball teams for 8-to-12-year-olds had expanded so rapidly that teams for older boys couldn't cope with the larger numbers of young men who had outgrown Little League. The greatest drawback in the city was lack of diamonds.

The phenomenal interest in baseball in Williamsport had not gone unnoticed elsewhere. Little League was now receiving international attention. The *Sun* writer observed that "throughout the United States, leagues patterned after Stotz's brainchild are springing up like weeds in a flower bed."

It was true. Little League had received considerable media exposure beyond Williamsport in 1946. It was also true that several newly formed leagues in and near Williamsport were patterned after Little League. Both the explosion of coverage in the media and the proliferation of Little League-like organizations nearby and far afield held promise for the future.

Lycoming Dairy Team, one of three i the first Little League in 1939, Managed b Carl E. Stotz. Kneeling: Major Gebror Dick Smith, Al Yearick, Jimmy Gebror Standing: Fred Sander, Tuck Frazier, Bi Bair, Ralph Mulenberger, Max Mille (Photo courtesy of Karen Stotz Myers)

Jumbo Pretzel Team, managed by Bert Bebble, was the second team of the first Little League teams to be sponsored. Kneeling: George Spooner, Bob Myers, Dick Preston, Ray Best, George Meck; Standing: T. Hinaman, Chas Zerbe, Leland Thomas, Bob Sahm, George Keys, Stan Keys (Photo Coutesy of Karen Stotz Myers)

Lundy Lumber, last of the first three Little League teams sponsored, was managed by George Bebble. Kneeling: Bob Smith, Maurice Reeder, George Fortner, Pete Smith; Standing: Pete Evans, Frank Sipe, Louie Langley, Noonie Smith, Don Kelly (Photo courtesy of Karen Stotz Myers)

The first specially built Little League field at Demorest Street and Memorial Avenue where Ralph Stotz used his car to help uproot small trees and stumps in the summer of 1939. (Photo courtesy of Karen Stotz Myers)

Joe Cardamone shook hands with each opposing team member who hit a home run during the 1948 World Series, providing Carl with his fondest memory, the perfect example of good sportsmanship. (Photo by Cleon C. Myers)

Little League Personnel, 1947: (left to right) front row-Oliver Fawcett, Howard Gair, Clyde Clark, Bert Haag, Vance Gair; back row: Martin Miller, Carl E. Stotz. John Lindemuth, William "Mac" McCloskey (Photo coutesy of Karen Stotz Myers)

Howard Gair became our head umpire in 1942, officiating an incredible 495 games over 15 years. (Photo by P. Vannucci)

William "Mac" McCloskey, longtime scorekeeper for the first Little League and innovative contributer to field facilities, shown announcing and scoring from the press box in the summer of 1946. (Photo courtesy of Karen Stotz Myers)

Little League Field in 1942. (Photo by Cleon C. Myers)

The legendary Cy Young enjoys a laugh with the California team at the 1954 Little League World Series. (Photo by P. Vannucci)

World Series Little League play at its best.

"Little League baseball originator Carl Stotz, right, with Floyd Mutchler, and Mutchler's great grandson, 7-year-old Matt, together 53 years to the day after the elder Mutchler became the first sponsor of a little league team— Lycoming Dairy Farms. 57th person approached by Carl, Floyd is 98 in the photo made in April 1992. (Photo by Craig W Smith)

Chapter 11

Baseball for small boys had spread throughout Williamsport and beyond in 1946 with formation of four more leagues: the Brandon Boys League, Maynard Midgets, Lincoln Boys League, and Williamsport Sunday School League. Now, in 1947, virtually every youngster in the 8-to-12 age group in the city had a chance to try out for a uniformed, adult-supervised baseball team if he wanted to and his parents approved. This development left the adults in our league feeling very good. We saw it as a solid endorsement of our program.

Elsewhere, too, leagues were being organized. That spring, Howard and Vance Gair, John Lindemuth, Marty Miller, Ollie Fawcett, Bill McCloskey, Clyde Clark, and I accepted an invitation to a dinner meeting arranged by the organizers of a four-team league in Lock Haven. The new league, sponsored by the Elks, Moose, V.F.W., and Sons of Italy in that small city about 25 miles west of Williamsport had a president, secretary-treasurer, statistician, and player agent. Harry German, a friend of mine since childhood, had brought the organization to this point following discussions with me the previous fall. The dinner was, in effect, a pep rally for adult personnel, sponsors, parents, and other interested persons in anticipation of the league opening that June. Three representatives from the adjoining borough of Mill Hall monitored the meeting with the hope of forming a league there.

Our Little League personnel were eager to share the expertise we had attained over the league's eight-year history. Each of us spoke briefly and answered questions.

The *Lock Haven Express*, the city's daily newspaper, reported that I had "outlined the entire setup, from the very first call for candidates to the final series and championship banquet." Miss Rebecca Gross, editor of the *Express*, became one of the movement's most enthusiastic supporters and a warm personal friend.

What was happening in Lock Haven was happening elsewhere. In Perry County, the Susquehanna River boroughs of Duncannon, Marysville, and Enola entered the picture. I was invited to speak to a group of interested adults from the three communities. The result was the development of the three-team West Shore Midget League. Each of the teams was sponsored by the Lions Club.

In the meantime, Montoursville and Milton, Susquehanna River towns near Williamsport, set up leagues for their youngsters. Nearby Montgomery had set up a league in 1946, which was the first patterned exactly after the Little League model developed in Williamsport. Jersey Shore, another nearby community, had baseball for small boys as early as 1940, but its program had little similarity to the Little League structure and mode of operation.

In 1947, I also advised a number of other communities in person and, still more, by mail. One community was Denver, near Reading, in southeastern Pennsylvania. That small community was so excited about baseball for boys that it had already invested $10,000 to provide a field complete with lights before it approached Little League for details on how to proceed.

One of the first leagues outside Pennsylvania closely patterned after ours was the Little Big League in Hammonton, New Jersey. Herb Juliano, one of its organizers, had come to Williamsport in 1946 to survey our setup for himself. When someone told me a man was on our field with surveying equipment, I went down to see what was going on. Herb was carefully checking the layout of the field and taking down measurements. The Hammonton League's managing personnel set lofty standards for their players during their initial season in 1947, providing adventure far beyond their expectations.

Thanks to Ray Rice, a former Eastern League catcher who had learned about Little League in 1942 when he was in Williamsport as a player for the Albany (New York) Senators, organized baseball for small boys was soon an ongoing program in East St. Louis, Missouri. Rice had left professional baseball at the end of the 1943 season and started a Jaycees' Baseball League for boys in 1944 as a member of the East St. Louis Chamber of Commerce. Then, in 1947, after the Jaycees' League had been functioning well for three years, the United States Junior Chamber of Commerce began promoting the program among all its chapters. Rice's success in East St. Louis made him the obvious person to direct the program nationally. Later, the Jaycees dropped their promotion of baseball for small boys in favor of the Little League program. Bill Kehoe reported in 1947 that Rice, the sports-and-recreation secretary for the National Junior Chamber of Commerce, planned to duplicate the Williamsport Little League program in East St. Louis. Kehoe had predicted that "some sweet day the Little League will become [a] national institution." His prophesy was coming true.

Baseball in the Little League mode was obviously beginning to catch on in the immediate post-World War II years, especially along the Susquehanna River. In 1954, *The Official Encyclopedia of Little League Baseball*, edited by Hy Turkin, reported 12 leagues in 1946, all in Pennsylvania, and 17 in 1947.

Little League was to see the 1947 season as a great turning point for the game it had begun and pioneered. From that year on, the climax of the season would be a tournament in late August to determine the champion of all the Little Leagues. The idea of such a tournament developed over a period of weeks; it was not a full-blown idea at first, but a result that came as we followed up on more modest intentions.

That spring, Little League had turned down an invitation to take part in an elimination tournament to determine the city champion among the 8-to-12 year-olds at the end of the season. In doing so, we were out of step with the Brandon, Maynard, and Lincoln Leagues.

At the time, no one had given any thought to a national tournament. In retrospect, it is obvious that our naiveté, more than anything else, made it possible. We weren't sophisticated enough to know that it was supposed to take a lot more planning to set up such an event successfully.

Our league had opened the 1947 season in the usual manner on June 4 at Max M. Brown Memorial Park. One hundred and sixty-six boys tried out. Those who failed to win positions in Little League were assigned to teams in our Minor League to develop experience to graduate to Little League.

As in each previous season, we worked tirelessly to improve facilities for both players and fans. We knew we were no longer unique in our endeavors, for adults in other small-boy leagues were now performing similar services for their players and fans. Mac engineered the laying of new underground electrical cables to center field for the larger sound system and the larger scoreboard he had designed and installed. We put in 120 feet of underground copper tubing to supply water for grooming the infield before games. For special guests, we built a concrete box-seat section and bought 18 folding chairs for their comfort. My Grayce, and Helen Fawcett, painted the bleachers and outfield fence and made 45 more cushions for game-time loan to the league's female fans. We also bought an additional 56 cushions that year. To the extent that imagination, time, and finances permitted, we strove to make our ball park the best possible.

Lycoming Dairy began the season as though in a class by itself. By winning five of its first six games by shutout, it outscored opponents, 54-2, easily winning the first half. It appeared as if there would not be much of a season for the other teams.

However, as we had done from the beginning in 1939, we played the season in halves, with each half being a new beginning. Lundy Lumber seized the opportunity as the second half began and, for a time, led the league.

Bill Avery, an 85-pounder in his last season of eligibility, was the Lundy Lumber team's secret weapon. He was the only pitcher in the league who consistently stilled the powerful Lycoming Dairy bats. At the same time, he was the most powerful hitter in the league, blasting out a record-setting 10 homers that season.

Bill's second victory over Lycoming Dairy, on July 19, was the most memorable of his career. Young Bill was scheduled to pitch that night, so his mother gave him his dinner and prepared to send him off early. Since the Averys were entertaining an elderly out-of-town guest for the evening, she told Bill, "When we come up, we'll park behind the left-field fence so Mr. Bacher can sit in the car to watch the game."

"You'd better not," warned Bill, remembering the

four balls he had hit over the left-field fence earlier in the season. "I might hit the car." Despite Bill's concern, when the game got underway, the Averys and Mr. Bacher watched from the comfort of their car, as planned. From there, they applauded Bill's homer in the third inning as it landed near the car.

Bill was becoming more and more concerned. In the fifth inning, as his team took the field, he asked left-fielder Dave "Snooky" Martin to tell Mr. Avery to move the car.

The car was still there when Bill stepped up to the plate for his last time at bat.

" "Yep," recalled Snooky Martin years later, "in those days the windshields were in two sections and the ball hit right on the metal strip in the middle and broke both sides."

"Bill Avery of Lundy's owes his father a new wind shield for the family car," wrote a local reporter the next day, "but Bill's father isn't complaining." He had been warned!

The second half of the season ended in a Lundy's-Lycoming tie for first place. In the three-game playoff to determine a clear-cut winner, Lycoming came out on top, 2-1, and was thus the 1947 league champion.

We had reconsidered our decision limit play within our league that year and allowed our boys to continue their play. Lycoming then swept a best-of-three series with an all-star team selected from the other three teams. After the first national tournament, the Lycoming Dairy players completed a five-game series against Armor Leather, champ of the Lincoln Boys League, winning it with a three-game sweep. They played the last game on August 29. Just as that series was ending, the league chartered a bus for a September 1 game in neighboring Lock Haven between their All-

Stars and ours. The big news wasn't Bill Avery's 10-strikeout shutout of the Havenites; it was the fact that everybody was reluctant to end the season.

The Brandon League champions, L. L. Stearns, sponsored by a city department store, defeated the Maynard League champ, V.F.W., in a seven-game series. Of the 17 teams playing Little League baseball, only the Williamsport Sunday School League Champ, Messiah Lutheran of South Williamsport, missed out on postseason, inter-league competition.

During the summer the newspapers had given ample attention to such Little League feats as Jim Sennett's 10-0 no-hit, no-run game, the first in the league since 1943 and only the third ever in Little League at that point. Jim's identical twin, Ed, was his battery mate. At the end of the season, Ed had his own moment of glory when the papers headlined him as the league's best batter with a season average of .473.

In what was to become somewhat of a stereotypical photograph in later years, a *Sun* photographer caught Dick Hayes of Lundy Lumber blowing a big bubble as he took a hefty swing at a pitched ball. Little League, however, was no longer the sole focal point of media attention. An exhibition at Bowman Field between teams from a new league led one reporter to note that this league was flying pennants over its field reminiscent of the pennants flown over the Bowman Field grandstand. In both instances, each pennant represented a team in the league.

With so many adults and entire families involved, fan interest was strong. Interest in the small boys' leagues, probably because of the uniqueness of their setups, even affected attendance at adult amateur games. In one instance, it was reported that a game in Brandon Park outdrew a nearby adult-league game with ". . . a larger attendance (much larger) than the . . . encounter on the nearby hardball diamond."

Not all spectators were supportive of the boys, however. Some seemed unable to see the games as simply little boys having fun in a structured, well-supervised athletic program. They behaved badly in response to what they took to be poor play or bad judgment. We in supervisory roles had to grapple with some of that. We tried to educate fans to the fact that we welcomed encouragement through applause and cheers but felt raucous criticism out of place at our games. The newer leagues were struggling with the same problem.

An editorial expressed concern at the growing number of incidents of booing at games involving 8-to-12-year-olds. After all, many of the boys had played less than a year. There was certainly no valid excuse for such adult criticism. And it was becoming quite discouraging to some of the boys. The columnist concluded what I have always believed to be true, that nothing but harm comes from such behavior. He said what more and more folks were saying by their participation, that the formation of the boys' leagues throughout the city was "the finest thing that could have ever happened to the kiddies in our city."

Fortunately, the booing fad of 1947 faded out, though the misguided enthusiasm for denouncing players, coaches, and officials remains a constant thorn-in-the-flesh wherever athletic contests are held. The fact that the vast majority of adults actively involved in Little League through the years has provided exemplary leadership for the youngsters has generally enabled the kids to shrug off the abusiveness of the occasional loudmouth on the sidelines.

Chapter 12

With the after-game improvement work at our ball park in 1947 well in hand by early July, we treated the players and ourselves to nonbaseball recreation. For several evenings we involved the boys, a team at a time, in miniature golf at the nearby Memorial Park course. I don't remember that we were consciously acting on the fact that many of the boys would finish their baseball careers when they were graduated from Little League. However, in retrospect, it is clear that certain of our extracurricular activities helped point them to interests other than baseball.

During the more relaxed period after our major field improvements were finished that summer, Ollie suggested that we take in one of the games in the newly formed Brandon Boys League. Since 1945, when the war finally ended, equipment became more available, and interest in forming Little Leagues grew in other areas of Williamsport and beyond. Both the Brandon League organizers and parents from Montgomery had asked me how to proceed.

Having read and digested all the organizational materials our league could provide, E.S. Frymire asked, in behalf of the Brandon League, if I would accept the presidency of a citywide organization of boys' leagues at the end of 1946. I declined, explaining that I hoped that each league would become an independent, self-governing organization operating within a defined neighborhood. Although my associates and I were eager to share what we had learned in our eight years of experience, we firmly believed the purpose of a league could be best served through a governing body made up of the men actually involved at the diamond level of operation. My response to Frymire was that a league should be the unit of organization, that each team should exist for competitive purposes only, and that the managers, umpires, player agent, and other operating personnel should be the governing body, with all decisions based on what was best for each league.

Naturally we, in what came to be known as Original Little League, felt complimented that others who were both baseball-minded and interested in children liked what we were doing and wanted to duplicate it. We were overjoyed that we were providing the experimental lab that was leading to the opportunity for many boys in other areas to play carefully organized, responsibly supervised baseball scaled to their size and ability. The Brandon Park game was the first we had seen that wasn't between teams in our league, and we liked what we saw.

As Ollie, Helen, Grayce, and I walked through the park after the game, Ollie suggested that we try to arrange a game between one of our teams and the Brandon League. He thought it would be a new and worthwhile experience for the boys.

At our next game, I called an impromptu meeting of our adult personnel. All agreed that the boys would enjoy such inter-league competition. Right away, we began thinking of more than one game. Then came the questions. How would we work the games around our regular schedule? Which teams would we play? How would we handle transportation?

In our league, Lycoming had won the first half. Lundy's was battling Lycoming to take the second and force a playoff for the championship. We believed we had enough open dates in the schedule to accommodate rainouts and tie games and still finish regular-season play on August 9.

We ended our meeting without accepting or rejecting Ollie's suggestion. We all liked the idea, but we were uncertain how to proceed. We agreed to think about it a few days and then discuss it again before trying to act on it.

When we resumed the discussion, someone suggested that we invite all known Little Leaguers to participate in a tournament at the end of the regular season. We recognized and discussed the responsibilities we would have as host league. Our personnel were willing to prepare the field, umpire the games, clean up, and do whatever else was necessary within the limits of their free, after-work time. The seed Ollie had planted was rapidly germinating into an exceptional plant.

Because I was routinely in direct contact with the adult personnel of new leagues as they came into being, I took on the job of arranging for and generally organizing the end-of-season tournament. In Grayce's longhand, records still exist of tournament regulations she later typed and mailed, injury waivers, game schedules, trophy orders, and all other tournament correspondence. She had everything in the mail a month before the August 22-23 tournament time.

I wrote to 15 leagues, including the local ones, about our round-robin-tournament plans and kept the newspapers informed. There had been some hard feelings when Little League refused to participate in citywide inter-league tournament play. Now with the round-robin tournament Little League was sponsoring, we hoped that would be put to rest. Reflecting the intense interest in Little League play at that time, 12 leagues returned entry forms. That was more tournament participants than we had anticipated, so we changed the starting date to the 21st.

To assure that so big an event for Little League players would run smoothly, we tried not to overlook anything that would add to the comfort and enjoyment of the boys. I contacted prospective umpires who could serve during daytime hours. The city's Eastern League team, then a Detroit farm club known as the Williamsport Tigers, under Bob Steinhipler, general manager, allowed us to use nearby Bowman Field lockers and shower rooms. Calvary Methodist Episcopal Church, three long blocks east of the field, served the meals.

More and more folks in Williamsport were beginning to lend support to Little League, from local theaters to the YMCA. The Pepsi-Cola Company and Dick Confair of Confair Bottling, my boss, picked up the tab for the champion's trophy. Two other companies, Capitol Bakers and Grit Publishing Company, paid for the runner-up and consolation trophies.

Now that we had so many participating leagues, we had to make decisions governing the makeup of tournament teams. Should participating leagues send their 1947 champions or league all-star teams? Our experience with the all-star teams of 1943 and 1944 had been good. As a result, we permitted leagues to send either their league champions or their all-stars, with the provision that each player must have played in at least 75 percent of the team's games during the season.

Though some involved in the expanding program continued to question the use of all-star teams instead of league champions for tournament representation, I consistently favored the all-star teams. Because the all-star teams were a combination of each league's best players working together for a common cause, the competition was heightened. Not only that, more of the 12-year-olds, in their last year of Little League, were able to participate. The playing field was leveled a bit more when the all-stars from areas of lower population density fielded their very best against the all-stars from the cities.

Totally committed to making the tournament a major event in Williamsport, I developed an eight-page program complete with league histories, a rundown on the players, and team photos. We printed 2,000 and could have used more.

Chapter 13

Heavy showers the afternoon of August 21 made the first day of the first annual Little League Championship Tournament one to remember. Original Little League, as some of us were beginning to call our organization, and the Sunday School All-Stars took the field promptly at 12:45 p.m. The boys played closely competitive ball into the bottom half of the third inning under threatening skies, with Original holding a 1-0 lead. When a steady downpour forced Umpire Sid Milnor to call the players off the field, the fans scurried for their cars and any other shelter they could find while the players sat it out in the dugouts.

Anticipating an end to the rain and an opportunity to continue the day's four-game schedule, if we could keep the field in playing condition, I went to the nearby Lundy Lumber Company and asked for a truckload of dry sawdust. Lundy's promptly loaded a truck and delivered it to the field. As soon as the rain stopped, we used the sawdust to soak up the water in the puddles so we could resume play.

The 40-minute delay changed the rhythm of the game, for in the fourth inning Original Little League led, 9-0. The final score was 15-0.

Before Lincoln Boys League and Montoursville could get the second game underway, another shower struck. When it became clear that at least two games would be rained out, I got the team managers together and rescheduled the rained-out games for the next afternoon on the Lincoln League diamond, about a mile away.

My chief assistant during the tournament was 11-

year-old Ernie Derr. Ernie lived a block up the hill from my house, just outside the boundaries of any of the leagues. Ernie and I had a special friendship which became even more special when his father was killed in an accident at a local steel mill. I knew that helping me would help him work off some of his grief, so I offered him the position. Like a shadow, Ernie followed me around, clipboard and pencil in hand, taking notes and reminding me of the things I needed to do. He even acted as official Little League emissary to the boys from Hammonton, New Jersey, escorting them to dinner the night they came in.

An hour or so before their arrival, Lew Carpenter of Jersey Shore, 12 miles to the west, and I were in telephone contact. Showers had hit Jersey Shore, too, and Lew was uncertain whether to bring his team to Williamsport for the 6:15 game. Optimistically, and perhaps because I didn't want any more rainouts if we could possibly avoid them, I advised him that the showers seemed to be letting up and the field was draining nicely. I thought we could play the game as scheduled.

Lew's contingent arrived in ample time for his boys to take warmup along with the opposing Maynard Midgets. It was their misfortune, however, to be up against the 10-strikeout, one-hit pitching of Don Stover and a lineup of good hitters. The Jersey Shore boys became the first team to fall prey to Maynard. The score was 8-1.

Both before and after the evening game, Howard, Vance, Johnny, Mac, Marty, Ollie, Clyde, and Bert devoted themselves to seeing that the field was in tiptop shape and the surrounding area thoroughly cleaned up. We were a proud group, and it showed.

We tried to think of everything to insure that tournament players and their adult personnel had a good time. I devised a system of team hosts, once again enlisting men from the community who gave so freely of their time. The hosts guided the teams around town in search of food and recreation. The team-host system proved so practical and popular that we made it a permanent part of all future tournaments.

All umpires were men recruited from local leagues and included a former Canadian-American League catcher. For the six opening-round games, we assigned two umpires per game and three umpires for quarter- and semifinal-round games. We added foul-line umpires for the championship game. Of the 10 umpires who worked the series, six were from Original Little League.

By using the Lincoln Field as well as Original Little League Field, we made up the rained-out games and completed the regular schedule on Friday, August 22. The lineup at Lincoln Field looked like this: Lincoln defeated Montoursville, 7-2, and Brandon Boys League took Montgomery, 4-2. Hammonton, New Jersey, edged out Milton Midget League, 6-4, and Lock Haven, with a four-run fifth inning, eliminated West Shore, 8-6.

The second round could have consisted of three games, there being six teams still in the running. That, however, would have necessitated a bye in the third semifinal round, which would have resulted in only two games on the final day of the tournament. The specific reason for granting byes to Hammonton and Lock Haven in the quarter-final round was to avoid having to grant a bye in the semifinal round and thus a pass into the final or championship game. In future years, the number of tournament teams never exceeded eight, so we no longer needed to grant byes.

As the boys from New Jersey and Lock Haven sat on

the sidelines, Lincoln took an immediate three-run lead and was never headed as it downed Original Little League, 7-4. Brandon, likewise, jumped off to a three-run lead against Maynard, but Maynard tied the game in the second and went on to win, 10-4.

With better weather, the number of fans increased and extra seating was brought in by the Williamsport Department of Parks. Armchair fans stirred up by press and radio coverage of tournament activities and fans who had attended earlier games showed up in force on August 23. A large crowd was on hand when Hammonton and Lock Haven took the field at 1 p.m. for the first of two semifinal games. Lock Haven took an early lead, scoring two runs in the first inning and adding another in the third. Hammonton scored its sole run in the top of the fifth on a home run. In the bottom of that inning, Lock Haven added two more to their score, winning the game, 5-1. Lock Haven's opponent in the final round was yet to be decided.

Both Maynard Midget League and Lincoln Boys League players were determined to win a place in the championship game. Consequently, their meeting in the semifinals produced the best-played game of the tournament. Lincoln scored a run in the top of the second. Maynard matched it in the bottom of the fourth. Tied 1-1 at the end of the regulation six innings, the teams played on even terms through the ninth inning, with neither scoring. A fielding error, a walk, and a single, after one man was out in the bottom of the tenth, brought in a run for Maynard and a 2-1 victory. In pitching his team to victory, Don Stover struck out 19. No other game in the series had so much drama and suspense.

For the championship game at 6:15, an estimated 2500 fans thronged Little League Field. Local newspapers termed the assemblage the largest crowd ever to witness an amateur athletic event in Williamsport. Certainly no previous amateur baseball game in the Williamsport area had aroused such widespread interest or brought out so many spectators.

Shouts of encouragement and vocal approval of fine play on the field couldn't help inspiring the boys to do their best. How often is anyone surrounded by so many known and unknown friends eager to see him excel? In this case, the Lycoming Creek dike, behind the outfield fence, became an extension of the bleachers and seating space for hundreds of people. Little League banners flew, fans waved tournament programs, and an aura of excitement and goodwill pervaded the park. Mac contributed with his precise announcements over the public-address system and his interspersing of appropriate music between innings. We wanted everyone who participated in or attended the tournament finale to remember it with pleasure and satisfaction.

Having been held to six singles and a double in the afternoon game, the Maynard Midgets, managed by Charley Scudder and Harry Berry, came out swinging in the championship game. Leadoff-hitter Tony Ingersol, outstanding batter of the series with a .625 average, went four-for-four. In four games, he had 10 hits in 16 times at bat. His teammates punched out 11 more hits. Lock Haven, managed by Ralph Condor, John Sebulka, Harry German, and John Poole, fought back valiantly. Although out-hit 15-8, the team never conceded until the third out in the bottom of the sixth, when Maynard became the first national champion, with a 16-7 victory.

Immediately after the game, I strode onto the infield and introduced the dignitaries who had agreed to present the various trophies and medals. Once all of the trophies were handed out, Mitch Younken, president of the Newberry Lions Club, presented an inscribed gold medal to each player of the championship team. Later, we inscribed a bronze medal for every boy who had taken part in the tournament. No youngster in the first National Little League Baseball Championship Tournament went home without a memento of his once-in-a-lifetime experience.

Little League Baseball continued to generate activities, displays, and newspaper copy for some weeks after the first national tournament. Maynard Midget League shared its national-championship trophy with all the kids within its boundary by displaying it in the four schools its players attended.

During the tournament, Associated Press had requested information from its Williamsport member newspapers and carried stories on its wires. Central Press, a national syndicate serving 700 newspapers, distributed a story and pictures of the tournament. People across America were beginning to hear about Little League through the media. Bill Kehoe continued to write that the tournament could grow to national proportions. He cited AP and CP coverage as proof of its news value.

Prophetic was the lead in a Williamsport newspaper item, shortly after the first tournament, which said it had the makings of a sports event of worldwide note. It suggested that the tournament would grow so large that it would have to be moved to a larger stadium, where admission could be charged.

In later year, when the tournament became known as the Little League World Series, it was moved to a site developed especially for it, the Howard J. Lamade Memorial Stadium in South Williamsport. [In 1992, a crowd estimated to number 40,000 turned out for the champion-ship game.] To its credit, Little League has continued our tradition of never charging admission to its games. It has also continued our tradition of accepting voluntary contri-butions from the fans.

To help build up the kitty to cover increasing costs as the Little League program grew, Henry Clifton, a photog-rapher, took many pictures during the first national tourna-ment and later sold them in the communities that had fielded the teams.

That championship tournament also introduced a young man who would gain a place for himself in American sports. Jack Losch, Maynard Midget's fleet center fielder, was an outstanding punt receiver in the late fifties and early sixties for the Green Bay Packers of the National Football League.

Chapter 14

Hardly had the first national tournament ended than I began anticipating a greater one in 1948. The first had brought together 11 teams from Pennsylvania and one from New Jersey. I intended to limit future national tournaments to eight teams, each of which, I hoped, would represent a different state.

If the vision I had was to become a reality, new leagues would have to catch on in rapidly escalating numbers. If that were to happen — and my increasing correspondence suggested it might — I needed better facilities to deal with it. My basement was the best place to begin.

I had built a recreation room years earlier, hoping I'd have the leisure to enjoy it. However, my involvement in Little League had become so time consuming that I needed a bigger office to handle all the interest and correspondence it was generating. I, therefore, eliminated the Ping-Pong table in favor of a desk.

My improvised office was a big asset. In it, I initiated and answered many letters in behalf of Little League. I developed our plans, wrote promotional material, and kept a file of our records. Because my time was limited, I answered many a letter at lunchtime or late at night at my basement desk. A little later, when the demand became even heavier, I added a mimeograph machine to speed up printing and mailing of materials.

During this period, the managing personnel of our Little League wore many hats. They coached, umpired, and did whatever was necessary in governing and running our league. They also set policy for the Little League Tournament Association.

When they met at our house January 3, 1948, I asked them to consider reorganizing to make the presidency of Little League an elective office. After discussing the matter briefly, they decided that inasmuch as the league had been operating successfully for nine years with the founder as president, I should continue in that office.

By this time, I was also able to report progress toward recruiting a sponsor for our national tournament. But, the major significance of that January 3, 1947, meeting was our decision to ask an attorney to meet with us as we considered whether to form a nonprofit Little League Corporation.

During this period, I had continued to encourage the formation of new leagues. When I came upon a copy of the 1947 National Baseball Congress yearbook, which not only covered all the activities of all affiliated nonprofessional leagues, but also included accounts of their most noteworthy leaders and active organizers and their addresses, I quickly got busy writing letters about the Little League program I envisioned for the future.

The write-ups impelled me to contact four of the men, one each from Connecticut, West Virginia, Ohio, and Delaware about the Little League program and my hopes for the future. How many of them answered my letter, I no longer remember, but at least one did. Bernard F. O'Roarke of Middletown, Connecticut, asked for more details and brought together an organization that fielded a league in 1948.

The Middletown league had one immediate distinction: it was the first such organization in Connecticut. Five years later, Joey Jay, an alumnus of the league's first season, became the first former Little Leaguer to reach the majors.

He had been a switch-hitting first baseman in Little League and a pitcher in high school. Jay, only 17, was the National League's youngest player in 1953, and one of the biggest at 6-foot-4 and 225 pounds. In his first start in the majors, he threw a three-hit shutout for his team, the Milwaukee Braves, defeating the Cincinnati Reds, 1-0. The young pitching prodigy's full name was Joseph Richard Jay, Jr. By the time his career in the major leagues ended in 1966, he had pitched for two teams. His record was 99 wins and 91 losses. I can't help wondering how much Little League influenced his life.

In his enthusiasm for the Little League program, B.J. O'Roarke helped other leagues organize in Connecticut. When the overall program became Little League Baseball, Inc., in 1950, he was named a member of the first board of directors.

As recently as 1980, another of the men to whom I had written was involved in the national program as a district administrator. I met Pat Knight, of Dover, Delaware, that year when he came by to see a display of memorabilia from Little League's earliest years that I showed during Little League World Series week. I recognized the name on his lapel pin, and he remembered that I had written to him more than 30 years earlier. Unless memory betrays me, those four men were the only people I ever contacted to suggest they organize Little Leagues. Everyone else contacted me.

The program was soon growing so rapidly that just keeping up with it was all the challenge I could handle. Little League was constantly on my mind. Had I not had a considerate employer like Dick Confair, I probably would have lost my job. That's how much Little League had come to dictate use of my time. Dick, being a very community-

minded citizen, saw merit in what I was doing and gener-
ously allowed me to fit much of it into my working hours,
giving me time off and tolerating lunchtime meetings that
ran into early afternoon. I also enjoyed evening use of the
office and its equipment in behalf of Little League until I
had a good typewriter of my own.

Whether meeting face-to-face with prospective
organizers of Little Leagues or responding to their inquiries by mail, I did my best to be helpful. Along with the
technical information about playing rules, league operating rules, facilities, equipment, financing, and necessary
personnel, I tried to set the tone or atmosphere I thought
best for the boys.

As delicately as I could, I reminded inquirers that,
however able some of the youngsters were, their being in
baseball uniforms did not change the fact that they were
still little boys. I discouraged the use of adult leaders who
would not set a good moral example for the players. Thus,
I advised that former professional and semiprofessional
players should not be involved solely for their baseball
expertise; they had to have qualities that made them
worthy of being looked up to by the boys. If, for example,
their sole goal was winning and their foremost example
was chomping on a big chew of tobacco, they should not
be part of the operation. Skillful, knowledgeable coaching,
yes, but only if properly motivated. Otherwise, I advised,
they should go with novice leaders whose primary concern was the well-being of the boys.

I wanted Little League, wherever it was organized,
to provide healthful fun in an atmosphere of good sportsmanship and clean living for every boy who participated.

Convinced that the second annual national tournament was certain and that we had our financial backing in

order, I made hotel reservations for the 1948 championship games. I also announced the Keds Little League National Tournament. The correspondence I had been receiving led me to believe that we would have teams competing from eight different states.

I considered New Jersey, Pennsylvania, Connecticut, New York, Virginia, and Michigan certain to send teams. I believed Maryland, Massachusetts, Delaware, and Ohio were likely to provide the other two teams. The latter four were only possibilities at that point because few leagues were being organized in their states. As it turned out, only six states qualified with functioning Little Leagues in 1948. One of them, Florida, had not been on my list of definites or possibles on April 24. One of my "definites," Michigan, didn't field its first league until 1949.

As April drew to a close, I was hard at work planning the Pennsylvania State Little League Tournament. Since we needed a sponsor for the state as well as national tournament, I contacted George R. Lamade, publisher of *Grit*, and was given a guarantee that Grit Publishing Company would underwrite the state tournament.

It was a foregone conclusion that the state tournament would be held at Original Little League Field. Our Little League Tournament Association had never given thought to the possibility that it might be played elsewhere. We knew we had something extraordinary going and we wanted to do well by those who came to Williamsport to take part. By now, more than baseball was involved. There was the matter of community pride — and Little League pride.

April had proved to be a propitious month for me and Little League. Invited to the community of Dushore to outline the procedures for organizing a league, I was surprised to see a large number of children waiting for us in the churchyard of St. Basil's.

When I explained to Fr. Pete Alisaukas that I didn't usually let the children know of my meetings — so they wouldn't be disappointed if a league wasn't formed — he explained that they weren't there because of the meeting. Their mothers were preparing for a church dinner. I agreed then that the boys could sit in on our meeting.

Along with my presentation, I included a showing of Charles Noll's color film of Little League teams. Then I answered questions from the floor. When there were no more questions from the men and I was about to end the meeting, a youngster raised his hand excitedly.

"When will we start to play?"

Before I answered, I called him to my side and asked his name. That's how I met Douglas Toothaker. I told Doug I couldn't answer his question, that the men would probably talk some more after the meeting to decide whether to form a league.

At that point, Guy Baldwin stood up and said he was sure Laporte could field a team, if there were teams for it to play. Then Mr. Connelly of Dushore said he'd talk to his business partner and they'd probably sponsor a team at Dushore. The men agreed to keep in touch about interest in their areas, and the meeting came to an end. A little child I had initially thought should not be present had led them.

Several weeks later, Mr. Baldwin came to see me in Williamsport and explained the progress they had made, including the building of a playing field in Laporte. He asked whether Little League could bring a team to Laporte for a game with their boys to help stimulate more interest.

The exhibition game was played on Laporte's mountaintop Little League field, where, after evening games, deer can occasionally be seen feeding just beyond the outfield fence. The league that was formed embraced six small communities along an 18-mile stretch of rural mountain highway. With this league, men of Sullivan County adopted the original neighborhood Little League program and brought the same opportunity to play adult-supervised baseball to rural youngsters.

Significant as that development was, it was not as far-reaching as something else that grew out of that exhibition game at Laporte. Once the game was scheduled, Guy Baldwin's wife, Margaret, an English teacher and a freelance writer, invited E.H. Brandt, a senior editor of the *Saturday Evening Post*, who was vacationing at Lake Mocoma, to attend the game with them.

Erd Brandt was so impressed with the boys' play and the manner in which the contest was conducted that he proposed doing a full-length article on Little League for the following spring. During the national tournament that August, the *Post's* Bill Strout took excellent pictures and Harry Paxton wrote with power and insight about Little League. Paxton concluded, "Already the idea has captivated thousands of boys and men in hundreds of communities. This is probably only the beginning." That article in the *Post's* May 14, 1949, issue was the single most important promotional influence in the history of Little League baseball.

Sullivan County's contribution to Little League didn't end with the success of the *Post* article and the flood of inquiries it brought from all over America. Guy Baldwin, first president of the Sullivan County League, was named a district director. In that volunteer role, he helped other new leagues develop. With the Baldwins' twin sons playing in Little League, Peg Baldwin became a "true blue"

Little League mother. Her understanding of the values the program could bring to the youth and community, if properly conducted, led her to write an article on the subject for *Reader's Digest*. It appeared in the American, Canadian, and Japanese August 1951 editions. Soon after, Canadian and Japanese youngsters as well as Americans were playing Little League baseball.

Also in 1951, when a publisher proposed I write a book, I suggested that Peg do the actual writing. I knew she had the knowledge and ability to weave together incidents I had experienced and experiences told to me by men from many leagues into a readable book. Not only did her *At Bat With Little League* prove interesting and inspirational, it also proved to be an excellent guide for organizing and operating a league. It captured the universality of many Little League experiences.

It is no wonder that Sullivan County, Pennsylvania, occupies a special place among my memories of the early years of Little League.

As soon as I knew with certainty where in Pennsylvania new leagues had been organized as a result of contacts with me over the winter, I invited them to send representatives to a meeting in Williamsport. I solicited their suggestions on tournament play and planning. The result of our discussion was the establishment of eight districts in Pennsylvania. Each district winner would be eligible to play in the state tournament scheduled for August 18-21 at Original Little League Field.

It was agreed that each team in the state tournament would pay its own transportation, but the Little League Tournament Association would provide housing and meals for the teams until they were eliminated by defeat. We reviewed the Little League playing rules so that all would interpret them the same way.

Concerned that no team should gain unfair advantage through the use of oversize bats, we decided that before every game we would check every bat with a bat gauge for diameter and measure it for length. The tournament director would take possession of any nonregulation-size bats until after the game.

Joe McNerney of the Granville Township League, near Lewistown, offered an important suggestion for enforcing the rule that runners weren't allowed to leave the base until the pitched ball reached the batter. He wanted the umpire to drop a signal flag the moment a runner left too soon. That procedure definitely establishes the violation and makes imposition of the penalty easier for the offending player to accept.

During the meeting, I appointed a tournament director for each district to be responsible for organizing, scheduling play, and directing tournament operation. Each league president would be responsible, as his team progressed, to provide parents-signed injury-release and age-certification forms to the tournament director for each player on his team. Each tournament team was allowed 14 players, none of whom could be 13 years old before August 1.

In considering fan contributions at games, we worked out a detailed plan for fair distribution of the proceeds. We agreed that each team would receive an equal share for each game it played in district competition and what share of the gross would go to the tournament association.

With the local-league play, league playoff games, and district, state, and national tournaments all competing for my time, the summer of 1948 would have been a busy one even if I hadn't had a full-time job. There were also construction projects to occupy our time.

Imitating the procedure followed by the National Soapbox Derby in Akron, Ohio, I established eight two-man teams of "Uncles" to serve as guides, one pair being assigned to each tournament team while it was in town. Sam Kreigbaum, head of the Pennsylvania Railroad Company Athletic Association, accepted my invitation to recruit them. Sam had been head of the railroad's physical-fitness program during World War I.

Busy men in responsible jobs responded to Sam's call, volunteering to devote many hours arranging transportation and accompanying teams during leisure-time periods. The system was intended to provide maximum assistance to the boys and to symbolize the friendliness of Williamsport. I believe it achieved both goals.

Chapter 15

Having set the stage through a series of letters to two companies in New York City, I was ready in early December 1947 to press my effort to obtain national sponsorship. U.S. Rubber was one of two firms I planned to visit in search of guaranteed financial aid for our program. The other was Pepsi-Cola, with whom my employer, Dick Confair, had arranged an appointment for me.

My bus left Williamsport at 10 p.m., December 3, and wound through one town after another in Pennsylvania's hard-coal region, arriving at the 60th Street terminal in New York at 6 a.m. After a light breakfast in the terminal, I studied the large wall map of the subway system to locate the offices I would be visiting. When I left the terminal, the air was so cold and windy it sent me scurrying down the stairway of the first subway station I came to.

I wandered through the maze of subterranean passageways enjoying the window displays, coming to street level only when I had to. Finally, I surfaced and found the Pepsi-Cola Company advertising headquarters on West 57th Street, where I had an 11 o'clock appointment. Next, I walked to Rockefeller Center to locate the office of the U.S. Rubber Company, returning in time to meet with Ruth Maier, a vice president in the Pepsi-Cola advertising department.

Miss Maier listened attentively, raised numerous questions, and was very gracious. She told me she would give me her decision if I would return that afternoon. My meeting with her improved my preparation for the unscheduled interview I hoped to have that afternoon with Charles Durban at U.S. Rubber.

When I arrived at Rockefeller Center again on my way to the U.S. Rubber Company offices, it was noon and skaters were gliding gracefully over the ice, creating a winter wonderland for the many onlookers. This fantasy-come-to-life gladdened the heart of the child within me, and sent me on the way to my destination in a festive mood. It was an ideal frame of mind to be in as I sought once more to advance my own particular fantasy in the world of reality.

Through correspondence, I had established contact with Thomas J. Young, U.S. Rubber's advertising director, and his assistant, Mr. Durban, who had been delegated to respond to my letters. Mr. Durban had asked for more specifics about Little League — expansion possibilities and projected cost of sponsorship. I had obtained a back issue of the *United States Atlas* and plotted distances between wide-ranging communities that I thought were the right size to organize and operate leagues. Then I estimated the probable expenses and projected the cost of tournament sponsorship. I mailed my reply, making sure Mr. Durban would have time to digest it before we met in his office. I hoped it would make my personal presentation of the many phases of Little League and plans for the 1948 national tournament more persuasive.

As I took the elevator to the sixth floor and waited in an outer office until Mr. Durban would see me, my enthusiasm began changing to anxiety. When Mr. Durban finally invited me in, his cordiality quickly put me at ease and restored my confidence. I was soon responding animatedly to his many questions about local leagues.

As I shared information based on my nine years of

firsthand experience in every aspect of league operation, his interest grew. He was amazed to learn how much time and effort the volunteers had given to help the pioneer Little League fulfill its purpose.

After I poured out my story and responded to his pointed questions for some time, Mr. Durban excused himself for a few minutes. He returned with Mr. Young. We shook hands and Mr. Young said Mr. Durban's briefing had made him want to meet me. He told me the matter of sponsorship would be completely in Mr. Durban's hands, then returned to his office. His confidence in Mr. Durban's judgment was encouraging, for I felt Mr. Durban was sympathetic to our Little League program and my projections for it.

As we continued our conversation, Mr. Durban told me that almost every week people came to his office to promote ventures of one kind or another. Usually, he said, the degree of merit he saw in any of them depended on the ability of the promoter once he obtained U.S. Rubber's financial backing. He added that, without exception, each promoter was trying to sell an idea that would put money from U.S. Rubber coffers directly into his pocket or provide other assured financial benefits. His question, then, was what personal financial consideration was I seeking.

Once more I explained that all of us in Original Little League were volunteers and were content to continue in that role. I sought nothing for myself from U.S. Rubber. My mission to New York was to find a sponsor to pay all team expenses for national-tournament players from the time they left their homes until they returned.

His response broadened my insight into the ways of big business, especially the built-in wariness against being sold a bill of goods. He was finally satisfied with my explanation and said he was convinced that I wanted nothing for myself but doubted that he could convince his superiors of that. He thought the best way was to take me to meet them face to face.

First on his list was Elmer White, a vice president. Mr. White demonstrated that human frailty is no respecter of position. A severe allergy that afflicted him aroused my pity and made me uncomfortable in his presence. While we chatted, he kept using one tissue after another from a box in the open top drawer of his desk.

Walter Norton, another vice president, also was a stranger to me, though his name was familiar. My dad and brother Ralph had often spoken of him when I was a child. He had been superintendent of the U.S. Rubber plant in Williamsport. In 1927, I had written a letter to him in behalf of Margaret Stotz, my maiden aunt, for 19 years a maker of galoshes for the company, who had been retired because of impaired sight. She had to cross the railroad switch tracks going to and from work, and the company feared she might fall and injure herself. In retirement, she hadn't cashed her pension checks and he wanted to know why. The uncashed checks were fouling up the company's pension-fund bookkeeping. It seemed that two of her elderly lady friends, both former U.S. Rubber Company employees who owned company stock, had told her the dividends on their shares were quite small. She mistakenly concluded her pension was the cause and sought to help by not cashing the checks. When I reminded Mr. Norton of Aunt Maggie's pension, he remembered it.

I also met Carlton Gilbert, another vice president. When I saw Henry Marlor's name on his office door, I was reminded of Marlor Hall, at Grier and Memorial Avenue in Williamsport. In 1918, when I was 18, Henry Marlor was superintendent of the Williamsport plant. The old mansion, named in his honor, had been a check-in point for company personnel transferred from New York.

The more people I met at U.S. Rubber, the more I felt that I was among friends. When we returned to his office, Mr. Durban gave me his decision. U.S. Rubber would sponsor the national tournament as I'd outlined it for him.

The purpose of my visit achieved, I brought up the concern that had led to my initial correspondence with U.S. Rubber. Little Leaguers needed better shoes than I could find on the market.

Sneakers weren't adequate, I explained, because they didn't provide enough traction for fielders when the grass was wet. On the other hand, steel-cleated shoes sized for boys were not a practical alternative. They constituted too great a risk of injury to infielders and base runners.

I suggested that a canvas-topped oxford with rubber-cleated shoes and a good insole that could approximate regulation baseball shoes would be exactly what we needed. U.S. Rubber agreed and, in 1948, designed and began the manufacture of the safe, practical, rubber-cleated canvas-topped shoes that became standard Little League footwear.

Four-and-a-half months after Durban assured me that his firm would sponsor the 1948 national tournament, we completed the arrangements. Certain of adequate financing — U.S. Rubber had pledged $5,000 — I breathed a lot easier as I planned and worked to make the second annual national tournament a vastly improved version of the first one.

While I was cooperating with U.S. Rubber to develop a Little League shoe, I also asked Spalding to make an official ball and Hillerich & Bradsby Company, manufacturers of Louisville Slugger bats, to make bats for Little League.

Spalding agreed to make a ball to Little League specifications and stamp it "Official Little League," if we could assure them a market. Harder's Sporting Goods Company of Williamsport provided that assurance by agreeing to buy Spalding's entire 1948 production of official Little League balls. Our specification was that they match the high-quality ball we'd used for the 1947 national tournament.

Our arrangement with Louisville Slugger for boy-sized bats was the same. Harder's agreed to take its entire production for 1948, 30 dozen, each stamped "Little League." Half measured 31 inches; half, 32. Half were of dark finish; half, light. The bats sold for $15.60 a dozen.

Before the season began, I sent out information on balls, bats, shoes, and league rules to all the leagues I knew of. Because official equipment was just being developed, I explained Harder's special role and suggested the leagues order balls and bats directly through that store. Actually, Little League bats were unobtainable from any other source in 1948. Once the market was assured, as I knew it would be, Spalding and Louisville Slugger would distribute the balls and bats through normal channels.

Harder's cooperation was commendable. They not only assumed the financial risk, but also agreed to ship stock to other sporting-goods stores as leagues requested the equipment.

Chapter 16

Our tenth season in Williamsport (1948) called for a special celebration. Hoping to enlist as many former Little Leaguers as possible and encourage their continuing interest in the game, the managers invited all who had been out of the league at least five years to meet with us to approve an electoral system for a Little League Hall of Fame. Within two days of our April 6 meeting, I mailed voting instructions to all of our 1939 players.

Though, at this time, our thoughts and efforts were frequently focused on the upcoming state and national tournaments, we had no intention of sacrificing our local program. We believed continuing to provide near-ideal opportunities for the boys in our league would serve as an example and guide to all the budding leagues across the country.

As a result, April and May tryouts were, as usual, a full opportunity for each boy to qualify. As always, we placed as many nonqualifiers as we could on minor-league teams to play in the Morning League and develop the skills that would help them succeed next season. We highly recommended this procedure to the scores of leagues getting ready to play their first season.

In our effort to do things right, we planned months in advance to open the season on June 2 with new uniforms. Ordering them in March, we believed they would arrive in plenty of time. When May 24 rolled around, I gave up waiting and called the company in Baltimore. I was assured they would arrive next day. When they still hadn't arrived as promised, and being truly dedicated and too worried to wait any longer, Marty and I got permission from the express company to hunt for our shipment. At 1:45 in the morning, May 26, with flashlights in hand, we entered the express car as soon as it was parked on the railroad siding. Coming up empty-handed, we resolved to return again next morning. Again armed with flashlights, we finally found the shirts. We only saved a day, but the relief of doing something about our predicament eased our growing tension and we breathed a little easier. Each manager got his team's uniforms that evening for distribution to his excited players.

True to tradition, our league began its season with two three-inning exhibition games. A good-sized crowd came out, representing an enthusiastic following for each of the four teams. On the next night, 250 fans showed up for the first regulation game of the season. They saw Bill Rosevear put on a power-hitting performance for Buick. With a homer and a double, he drove in five runs to lead his team to a 7-2 victory.

Whenever I could find time in early 1948, I devoted it to the preparation of a 25-page booklet of the year-by-year history of the league, including photos of the various teams. Connie Mack, longtime owner of the Philadelphia Athletics, had written in his book *My 66 Years in the Big Leagues*: "As baseball years are counted by seasons, anniversaries all come at the close of the season." But, I couldn't wait. The commemorative booklet was ready June 21, and I began distributing it immediately. Although I hadn't intended or expected it to be a fundraiser, it brought in contributions several hundred dollars above printing costs. In effect, we celebrated throughout the tenth season.

Like the previous season, this one was a running battle between Lundy's and Lycoming. Lundy's won the first half, and Lycoming narrowly won the second half in the final games. The championship playoffs went the full seven games, with Lundy's coming out on top.

Our Original Little League interrupted its championship series for one evening to permit the league all-star team to compete against Maynard Midget League, the 1947 national champion. The evenly matched teams battled in a scoreless tie until, with one out in the bottom of the sixth, Ray "Skip" Singley blasted a home run for the Maynard team. He had won his own game, pitching a two-hitter in which he had struck out six batters.

In the second and final round of District 1 play, Maynard fell to the heavy-hitting Lincoln League team, 7-4. Three Lincoln batters, Berfield, Jenkins, and Bachman, had hit home runs. Bachman, the pitcher, hit two. Lincoln was one of eight Pennsylvania district champs, each of which competed in the state tournament in August.

Whatever excitement the rapid expansion of Little League at district, state, and national levels was stirring up, we did not neglect our primary obligation to the boys of Original Little League. After their season ended, they enjoyed the traditional awards banquet. They knew, too, that their league was the successful model for all the leagues that were sprouting everywhere, and they felt good about that.

Our managing personnel had done a fabulous job with the league and with the tournament association in 1948, so it was fitting that we celebrate as the year ended. We had worked so long and so well together that we were really all one big, happy family.

Chapter 17

Well before the 1948 season began, we decided Original Little League Field would be immeasurably improved for state and national tournaments if we added a clubhouse-office-press box building. Planning the new structure and getting it erected was my responsibility. The project was more than we volunteers could take on unaided. We needed the expertise and skills of professionals. We also needed more money.

Unsolicited contributions had come to Little League over the last four years from organizations like the Williamsport Wheel Club. Often the contributions were followed with promises of support if and when we were in need. Confidently, I began to pursue our plans for further improvements. Although money was a major factor in our ability to complete our plans, it was the volunteers who really made success possible.

I found someone with a backhoe to prepare the construction site, bought shovels and paint brushes, and set to work.

Though our improvised home-run fence had served its purpose passably for several years, our current needs demanded something better and higher. Our taller boys would sometimes fall over the fence while attempting to catch long fly balls, so we added a fence to our list of things to build.

It was nearly the end of May, and our sense of urgency was growing. We had to be ready in time for the national tournament. That sense of urgency behind me for impetus, I approached the Williamsport Building Trades Council for professional help, outlining our plans for its members and requesting their assistance.

While I awaited the council's decision, I made

more-detailed drawings for the clubhouse I envisioned. With showers and a dressing room at field level and press box and office above, I had things pretty well planned out. But, not being a trained architect, I had my doubts.

Once again, a volunteer donated his time and energy to Little League. Architect W.D. Shollenberger drew up the plans, and volunteers from the Trades Council turned them into a building.

While professionals worked on one side of the field, the amateurs busily dug post holes behind the old fence on the other side. However, once we actually began to build the new fence, we realized we had to hire someone to complete the job, for the volunteers' work limited the time they could devote to it.

In July, Howard Cox painted advertisements on the fence, and our field took on the appearance of a major league stadium.

Still working on the clubhouse, volunteer umpires and managers hand-dug footings and ditches for water pipes while local electricians and plumbers continued to lend their support. Mac McClosky's improved center-field scoreboard with a new, concealed 24-inch loud speaker flanked by paintings of outfielders in action added to the aura of big-time baseball.

With the national tournament only four days away, the cement floor of the clubhouse hadn't been poured yet. But, we didn't panic; we hadn't time! We arranged for an early morning delivery of cement and finished putting up the last of our protective barricades by the time players began to arrive August 21 for the 2 p.m. consolation game of the state tournament.

Lacking time to finish the press box perfectly, we used the back of an old church pew as a tabletop for the sportswriters, completing our new newsroom in time for the national tournament.

Once the tournament was behind us, we resumed work on the main floor of the building. We hired a mason/carpenter to keep the work going. With Johnny Lindemuth's help, the work progressed well.

Dreaming, anticipating, hoping, planning, executing, I was up to my ears in each step where Little League was concerned. No sooner would one challenge, problem, or need be resolved than I'd take on another. On every side, I now had eager volunteer helpers, but I'm sure no one involved in our expanding program found more fun, excitement, and adventure in it than I did. It had virtually become my life.

I hoped to see Little League become as much of a national institution as the annual Soapbox Derby.

On field and off, I tried to think of every detail so that nothing would be left to chance. Even the uniforms for the 1948 national tournament were special. I planned that in each game one team would wear scarlet-trimmed uniforms; the other team, uniforms trimmed in royal blue. I wanted to show the U.S. Rubber Company how much their support meant to Little League by designating the blue team the U.S. Royals and the red team the U.S. Keds.

In effect, I was trying to follow the procedure we had had with sponsors of local teams from the beginning. I was therefore taken by surprise when an official of U.S. Rubber, in Williamsport for the tournament, said he feared such use of company trade names would imply that U.S. Rubber was exploiting the children, a criticism both undesirable and untrue. In the years thereafter, we used the names of states on tournament uniforms.

Chapter 18

With the 1948 tournament barely a month behind me, I was in New York again. Emerson Yorke was putting together a movie of the series and needed studio closeups of me and help identifying players.

The following day, I met with Charles Durban at the U.S. Rubber Company offices. His associates were pleased with what they had seen at the tournament, he told me, so pleased, in fact, that they were willing to provide funds for an assistant for me. I had been working too hard, he said, and U.S. Rubber wanted to help.

I explained my employment situation, that Dick Confair had been patient and understanding. I saw no need for a paid assistant. However, his offer set me to thinking about my situation and reviewing some facts. Eddie Richner had been Confair's office man when I was hired and, being of a younger age, was called for military service. Meanwhile, I was given greater responsibility and later named plant and office manager. When Eddie returned from the service, I felt uncomfortable being in the position he no doubt would have earned had he not been away serving his country.

Mr. Durban had other things to bring up. He guided the conversation to the Soapbox Derby and how General Motors had made a financial arrangement with Derby founder Myron Scott to become the event's controlling sponsor. Showing no particular interest in his observation, I said I did not want to be employed by U.S. Rubber Company. I wanted Little League to remain an independent entity. He then walked to a window in his office overlooking the Avenue of the Americas. Beckoning me to his side, he gestured toward the street below and said, "In those taxis rushing by, you will find drivers of varying backgrounds. You will find a man who is quite a philosopher, some who are victims of misfortune, some for whom the position represents the attainment of a goal, and even some who were inventors but let an opportunity slip away, to their later regret." I then offered to serve as national director of Little League for an annual fee sufficient to provide my livelihood. On that basis, Mr. Durban doubled his original offer, and subsequently an agreement was formally documented.

With our conference ended, I immediately drove to my brother Ralph's home in Naugatuck, Connecticut, to attend a meeting in Middletown to discuss the formation of Little Leagues. That meeting led to a number of new leagues in 1949.

Ralph had caught the Little League fever, too. The following morning he took me to look over an open field to lay out tentative plans for a ball diamond. Though two Middletown teams were granted permission to play an exhibition game there, permission to build was denied.

Undaunted, Ralph continued his search until he found another site. Though it was less than ideal, he and an energetic group of men turned that uneven, undersized field into the first Little League park in New England. When finished, it boasted a two-story clubhouse, press box, and locker/shower room, and was surrounded by bleachers. Ralph had unabashedly solicited free materials and the use of earth-moving equipment to build Peter Foley Little League Park. Dedicated in 1949, it was the finest facility of its era for small boys' baseball and a testimony to the dedicated volunteers who put it all together.

By the time I returned home that October, there

was a stack of inquiries looking for Little League information and invitations to speak about the Little League program. One look at the inquiries coming in in growing numbers convinced me that I needed to streamline my office procedures with prepared information packets ready to send as quickly as the questions came in. How I got anything done for Confair Bottling Company anymore must go down as at least a minor miracle. I was spending more and more time away from Williamsport.

Speaking engagements in Pennsylvania and New Jersey followed planning sessions. Looking for input only experience can provide, I also invited the presidents of all the leagues that had been 1948 Pennsylvania State Tournament participants to meet with me.

I also conducted my own survey to determine how many communities of 10,000 — the size cities I wanted to target in my promotional campaign — there were in the U.S. and in my home state. In 1948, there were 1,153 leagues nationwide and 108 in Pennsylvania.

Throughout November and December, I continued working with Emerson Yorke on the 1948 Keds National Little League Tournament movie. Never, in my fondest dreams, had I ever envisioned myself looking over the shoulder of the great film editor of *Lost Horizon*. But, there I was, identifying players and describing the play. My respect for the actor's craft grew considerably as I tried to deliver prepared lines to the director's satisfaction.

In mid-December, I was in Chicago to introduce U.S. Rubber Company Footwear Division representatives from across the country to the Little League program. Not normally a part of the corporate world, I was surprised when the young man assigned to steer me around and keep me on schedule asked to see the notes for my address. "I don't speak from notes," I told him. He insisted I have something for him, nonetheless, so I wrote an introduction on the back of my appointment book.

First, I talked briefly about the relationship between Williamsport, U.S. Rubber, and baseball. When Mr. Marlor was at the plant in Williamsport, the company began an expansion project using a popular baseball field/ cow pasture as a building site. That, of course, led to a scented story about the old days and sliding into what only looked like second base. But, Mr. Marlor understood our needs and provided another site. I figured that story would break the ice and I could go ahead and tell them about the Little League experience.

I was gratified by the questions that followed and the enthusiasm generated, but now I was concerned that soon there would be an army of uninformed "experts" shooting across the country in every direction. When I took my misgivings up with Mr. Durban, he assured me that all requests would continue to be sent directly to me. So far as I was concerned, that was the only way to insure that all leagues would be organized on the same basis.

Chapter 19

The early months of 1948 kept me constantly on the move spreading the message of Little League. Almost faster than I could keep up, communities asked me to help them develop their own Little League programs. Although caring for our daughters, Monya and Karen, limited Grayce's available time, she continued to handle the ever-increasing secretarial services Little League's exploding popularity required. Without Grayce's help, I wouldn't have had time for the many promotional trips throughout Pennsylvania and into nearby states.

Returning home euphoric from a successful 4,000-mile itinerary through the South, I was surprised to learn that the Little League I had envisioned and organized was upsetting to some people.

I had been invited to speak before two physical-education classes at nearby Penn State University. I began my program as usual, showing the Little League movie and making my set presentation.

The students watched the film as attentively as any group I had appeared before. However, not having attended college myself, I did not anticipated what was to follow.

Asked by their professor to respond critically to my presentation, students in every part of the room waved their hands. I was dumbfounded. It appeared that every student wanted to challenge what I'd said.

Although my purpose in promoting Little League and my understanding of how the game should be made available and operated for boys differed pointedly from what I was hearing, I listened with admiration as the students expressed themselves. They were perceptive, spotting potential faults and criticizing them as possibly dangerous to the health and welfare of Little Leaguers. I was silently thankful that in the 10 years since I had founded the sport, none of those fears had become a reality. I could not deny that for Little Leaguers there is always some risk, however remote. There are always risks in athletics, regardless of the athlete's age. But, I was confident that the high-percentage probability of physical or emotional injury some of the questions and comments suggested was not borne out by the 10-year history of Little League.

What surprised and disturbed me most was the strong antagonism that surfaced against volunteers. The students, training for careers in public recreation, questioned the qualifications of volunteers to direct Little League activities at the field level. They left me in no doubt that, in their opinion, it was unwise to have any but trained professionals in charge of any form of public recreation.

Amused at the blindness induced by the students' training, I reflected as I returned my equipment to the car that perhaps I had all along misunderstood the meaning of the word "recreation." Perhaps it no longer had the promise of "re-creation" in other than university-trained hands; it must now be considered "wreck-creation," a disaster waiting to happen.

A couple of months later, in Boston, Massachusetts, I learned that the students had anticipated their professional elders. I was a guest of the National Convention of the American Association for Health, Physical Education, and Recreation. Jack Kuhn of U.S. Rubber and Emerson Yorke, the movie producer, presented the recently completed sound movie of the 1948 Little League National

Tournament to a full hall. After the movie, the convention recessed briefly so we could all go outside and watch the Boston Marathon runners go by.

The break inspired me, for as I watched the hundreds of runners pass by — it was impossible to watch any single runner for more than a moment — I remembered a race in the districtwide annual elementary-school track meet in 1925. Harry German, the winner, was a small, frail looking lad from a small, township school just outside the city. I could still visualize him raising half a lemon to his mouth with measured regularity as he kept widening his lead over the rest of the field, leaving seemingly more powerful competitors in his dust. The memory of his victory encouraged me as I returned to the meeting room to field a host of critical questions.

I was not in Boston that day to promote formations of more leagues. I was there to answer the association members' questions and see that the information they received about Little League was accurate. With few exceptions, Little League had taken hold in community after community because some individual or small group wanted to provide it for the boys of their neighborhood. That had been my hope from the beginning. I wanted each neighborhood league to be separate and autonomous, and all leadership provided by capable residents of the community serving as volunteers. On that, I was resolute!

Most of the questioners seemed sincerely interested in learning more about Little League and how it functioned. However, the little speeches with which association members prefaced their questions indicated a reluctance to acknowledge that Little League was rapidly being accepted nationally as a healthful sports program for boys.

Had I not been involved in every aspect of field activity for the full decade of Little League's history, my role that day would have been painfully traumatic. As it was, I felt confident. Experience had been an excellent teacher. Question after question raised the specter of harmful effects that could result for boys who played in Little League. None, however, included firsthand information of actual situations to support their gloomy outlook. As on the occasion with the Penn State professor and students, I could not refute assertions of what might be possible, but I rejected the implication that the disastrous consequences they foresaw were probable.

Being highly educated in their field, most who rose to challenge me were quite scholarly in language and approach to the subject. They referred glibly to the authors of various studies and quoted from their reports. No doubt they were convincing to one another within their narrowly defined group. They were not convincing to me. My belief in Little League remained unshaken.

To put the issue in perspective, I asked them to acknowledge that boys were going to play baseball whether or not proper equipment and supervision were available. My point was that whatever imperfections Little League had, it was far better than the unsupervised sandlot games boys would play if Little League were not available to them.

What I could not understand then and cannot understand now is why well-educated people spend so much time speculating about remotely possible consequences of some minimally dangerous activity while virtually ignoring more serious proven dangers to people's health and well-being. Since early youth, I have been dismayed at the manner in which millions ignore the scientifically proven damage alcoholic beverages and ciga-

see me as an enemy. He saw me as a friend, which my associates and I had tried to be to every boy who tried out, whether he made a team or not. Jim's earlier disappointments had left no scars. Instead, it seemed to me, his Little League experience had contributed to his character with more positive impact than that which accrued to the outstanding players of the league.

Any Little League manager worthy of the position knows the disappointment boys feel when they are cut from the squad. If he keeps contact in later life, he will find that his considerate handling of the crucial cutting situation has not been deeply wounding and has left no lasting scars. A number of times over the years, former disappointed player candidates have asked me to accompany them to father-son banquets, to accept nominations for awards from their schools, or to accept honors from clubs they're in. I doubt that I am an exception in that regard.

Strangely, I do not remember a single champion pitcher, outstanding hitter, or other highly acclaimed player showing me such honor. Unless my experience is proved to be unusual, the lesson is clear: too much adulation of the individual champion is inimical to character development, and so the manager, league personnel, proud parents, and friends would do well to keep their acclaim of the heroes within reasonable bounds. Far better, it seems to me, is to help all the youngsters realize that their excellence on the field or off can be of continued value to the community. A champion becomes a role model to his peers and younger children, so he should be encouraged in every way possible to be a good example. That is one important reason why character building was an aim of Little League from the beginning.

Meeting with professional critics of Little League

and philosophizing about their negative attitudes actually took very little of my time. There were far too many positive opportunities bekoning. Free now from the limitations of earning a living at a non-Little League-related job, I gave my brainchild virtually every minute of my time.

My promotional appearances early in 1949 took me across central and southwestern Pennsylvania. To keep these early-March appointments, I traveled alone over hazardous icy roads in lonely mountainous country.

It was in Renovo, after a long, after-dark journey from Punxsutawney over a treacherous ice-covered highway through the State Forest Natural Area that I had one of my most rewarding experiences. One of the men present when I arrived for the 9 o'clock meeting was one of my boyhood heroes whom I had admired from a distance. Now I shook his hand for the first time.

Louie Bruno had been center fielder in 1921 when Williamsport defeated Pitcairn, Pennsylvania, to win the Pennsylvania Railroad regional championship. His "impossible" somersaulting shoestring catch had been the outstanding play of the game. The crowd that day was larger than any previous one at a ball game in Williamsport, and I was part of it. I was one of the nonpaying fans.

When I arrived at the ball field that day, the stands were filled and the vast overflow crowd was seated on the grass behind the ropes stretched around the outfield and along the foul lines. The confusion made it easy for a slight 11-year-old like me to slip in free. I simply pushed aside a loose board in the outfield fence and squeezed through.

My experience was totally positive at Renovo. The enthusiasm for organizing and developing the best league possible for their boys was impressive. I was later to learn in an unexpected way that they successfully followed the printed guidelines from our Williamsport headquarters.

I was stopped on the street in Williamsport by a truck-driver who laughingly told me what had happened the night his truck broke down in Renovo.

Because his truck couldn't be repaired, he'd had to take a room in the town's only hotel. As he was relaxing in the lobby with the evening paper, he heard an auction in progress in the adjoining meeting room. To his astonishment, he heard names and ages of boys announced, then other voices excitedly bidding. He could not believe what he was hearing — the men were buying young ballplayers!

Distressed at what seemed deplorable exploitation of children, he inquired about it. His shock turned to understanding and amusement when he realized how widely he had misinterpreted what he had overheard. The bids of 800, 1100, and so on did not commit dollars for the prospective players but credit points. The team managers had been using the system I had devised to compete fairly for players for their teams.

Naturally, I was pleased to learn that Renovo had accepted and used the official Player Selection System. The purpose of it from the beginning had been to provide the most equitable means possible for determining which boys should play on which team. Like an insurance policy, the system sought to cover all foreseeable situations. The intent was to give each candidate an equal opportunity, based on playing ability, to be selected for a team. Much of the success of the resulting teams depends, of course, on the managers' ability to evaluate a candidates' ability and to coach effectively. The goal for the players is to improve their skills and learn to play well together in an atmosphere of good sportsmanship.

Late winter and early spring of 1949 saw me in

Williamsport just long enough to plan new schedules and cram as much essential administrative activity as possible into a few days. Then I was off again, meeting with interested groups across seven states. In Canton, Ohio, I made my presentation before the Fraternal Order of Police of Ohio. The FOPO had sponsored a "Hot Stove League" for a number of years and was considering forming and operating a statewide baseball program for boys. Later, S.S. Courtney, my Canton host, told me my presentation had been the catalyst for changing their plans and encouraging each local chapter to decide for itself whether to organize a community Little League.

In the meantime, Courtney had actively campaigned for and organized a league in Canton, overcoming all obstacles, including the city recreation authority's objections.

My return to Canton March 7 brought results that led to a close friendship with Cy Young, who was already a baseball legend when I was a boy. When the newly established Canton league went into operation that spring, Cy Young's participation made its opening more auspicious than most. The elderly gentleman had traveled to Canton from his home in Peoli, Ohio, 59 miles away, to throw out the first ball. Young had begun his professional career in Canton in 1890. I met him again two years later and saw him annually after that.

There were other first-season openers in 1949 that were standouts for me. My brother Ralph's efforts in Naugatuck, Connecticut, resulted in an opening day the local paper described as one that would be remembered for years to come. I certainly wouldn't forget it. Ralph was working to put the finishing touches on the stadium the day before the opening. I could certainly appreciate the time it took. I was proud of Ralph and the men who built their stadium and made the league work.

I returned to Williamsport just long enough to report on Little League's progress before I was off to another memorable season opener; this time, in DuBois, Pennsylvania.

Jimmy Gehron was staying with me for the summer after high-school graduation in Knoxville, Tennessee, and was able to accompany me when I met A.P. Way, an 81-year-old Little League enthusiast, former state assemblyman, theater owner, and philanthropist who had built a Little League field for the youngsters in his comunity. His effusive welcome and the thrill the boys got from meeting Jimmy as one of the inspirations for Little League made the dedication of the A.P. Way Little League Field seem anticlimactic in comparison.

The year 1949 literally overflowed with rewarding events, both for me and for Little League. How could anything top it?

A seed planted a year earlier had germinated and grown, and in the May 14 issue of the *Saturday Evening Post* produced the tasty fruit we had hoped for. It was Harry T. Paxton's long article on Little League entitled "Small Boy's Dream Come True." A deluge of inquiries from all over the country flooded our Williamsport headquarters. Its impact was felt for years.

The *Post's* was the first in-depth treatment of Little League by a national publication with a big circulation. Besides being on the newsstands, the popular weekly went directly into the homes of 4,000,000 subscribers. Paxton's breezy style brought Little League alive to the *Post's* millions of readers in a way that run-of-the-mill newspaper articles could not. And, the timing of its publication could not have been better, for it came just as the 1949 season was about to begin.

It was impossible to help communities create instant leagues and enjoy a full season in 1949, but the response assured a virtual explosion of new leagues in 1950. As inquiries arrived, we stuck colored pins in a large map to note their locations and sent each inquirer a packet of Little League materials. By the time I planned fall league meetings, the clusters of pins on the map had grown so numerous that only by setting up meetings in central locations could I accomodate every community looking for help.

Television, too, had noticed Little League. On May 10, I made my first TV appearance, in New York City, during a 15-minute live interview on "Manhattan Spotlight." About two-and-a-half months later, Bill Stern, then one of the nation's most popular sportscasters, interviewed me on his TV program. In August, I was given a spot on "We, the People."

What I remember most fondly about the "We, the People" experience is Connie Mack's presence. Connie was then in the twilight of his long career as owner-manager of the Philadelphia Athletics. Young Fred Gallagher and Jack Stryker, whom I had taken along, were posed with the baseball patriarch. He sat with them on a bench, as if in a dugout, with water bucket and towel nearby. Over the years since, I have seen many copies of a painting of similar pose and have wondered whether the pose of Connie Mack and the boys on the TV program inspired the painting or whether the painting inspired the pose.

Chapter 20

Little League had become a hot topic, and I did my best to present it in the most positive way possible. Naturally, radio interviews were more frequent than television appearances, for television, like Little League, was just beginning to grow toward its great potential.

The print media added immeasurably to our exposure nationally. *Life*, the first and best photo-journalism magazine, followed the *Post* in publicizing Little League in a way that had great public impact. *Life's* coverage introduced additional millions to what was happening in Williamsport.

July 12, the day *Life's* photographers came to town, was a carefully planned day. We wanted them to have something exceptional to report in pictures. The occasion was the third annual Amateur Night of the Double A Williamsport Tigers. It was also Appreciation Night for the Williamsport High School Band.

Before nearly 5,000 applauding fans crowding the stands, the band, known as the Marching Millionaires, led a parade of 1,000 amateur baseball players around the field before the first game of a doubleheader. There were nine teams of Little Leaguers and teenagers and men of the older circuits. The amateur players, all in uniform, stood in formation on the infield grass while photographers shot pictures from the grandstand roof and from the raised ladder of a firetruck parked behind home plate.

Thanks to the wire services and news syndicates, newspapers around the country had frequent access to stories and items about Little League. Williamsport journalists placed occasional articles with house organs and other special-audience publications. Assisted by local newspaper morgues, I was the source of most of what they wrote. We had a common interest in promoting our baseball program as far afield as we could as rapidly as we could. We were proud that it was putting our city on the map as the birthplace of Little League and drawing thousands to our national tournament.

That was also the year Emerson Yorke brought his film of Little League baseball to Williamsport for its premier showing at the Capitol Theatre. U.S. Rubber Company officials mingled with community civic and business leaders, Little Leaguers and their parents, Little League volunteers, and representatives of the news media. The movie was an immediate hit.

For the principals in attendance, the evening was just beginning. In his inimitable striving for the dramatic, Emerson Yorke took charge. He hurriedly ushered us into limousines lined up outside the theater and took us on a police-escorted, high-speed ride to Lock Haven, about 30 miles up river. The wild motorcade was more an exhibition than a necessity. I know I was not alone in thinking we might be making an exit from this world rather than an entrance to Lock Haven. There were no seat belts in automobiles in those days, and it was Friday the 13th!

Lock Havenites certainly knew we had arrived as we pulled up before the Roxy Theater with sirens screaming. There was no way, however, that our noisy arrival could match the spontaneous welcome Lock Haven had given its Little Leaguers nine months earlier when they returned from Williamsport with the National Championship trophy. Nevertheless, the new movie was enthusiastically received there, too.

U.S. Rubber provided numerous copies of the film

for loan from Williamsport headquarters to communities that wanted to build interest in forming leagues. Seeing that films were kept in use was one of my self-assigned responsibilities, for my contract gave me authority to conduct the national program as I thought best.

Immediately, an average of one copy of the Little League movie was going out every day. Its popularity never left us in any doubt of its value as a promotional vehicle.

In mid-July, a family trip to Cooperstown, New York, became my most satisfying experience with the film. Jimmy Gehron accompanied us. Naturally, our first stop was the Baseball Hall of Fame. For a family more and more immersed in baseball, that alone made the trip worthwhile. Later, while the others were relaxing, I was on duty.

I met with the local school athletic director and Charles Durban, who had come up from New York City to present a copy of the film for Cooperstown to show during its formal baseball celebration. The high-school band played, I spoke as founder of Little League, and Mr. Durban introduced the film. It was thrilling to be in the town where baseball memories and artifacts attract fans worldwide.

Little League was my baby, and I was very protective of it; Mr. Durban was well aware of that. He also knew that others besides U.S. Rubber wanted a tie-in with me. When we met at Cooperstown, he sought my assurance that I would not make any commitments that conflicted with U.S. Rubber's interests in the program. I was pleased to know that the company was committed to long-term support of Little League and happily accommodated him.

The U.S. Rubber people I dealt with were pleasant, helpful people, and their interest in Little League was far more than casual. They were people who were as full of ideas about its future as I was.

About a month before my Cooperstown meeting with Mr. Durban, Jack Kuhn, another of U.S. Rubber's representatives, had a comprehensive discussion with me about Little League. Jack told me Mr. Durban had asked him to think about where the Little League program might lead. He had done so. Now he was carrying out the second part of his assignment, to meet with me and discuss his suggestions for the future.

Jack and I were friends in serious conversation as we sat at a card table in a shady area of my yard. He had brought some written material along, showing that he had spent considerable time and effort in preparation. That is pretty much the way I have always approached things. It impresses me when others are as meticulous about detail as I am.

I listened carefully to Jack's rather inclusive plan, not even interrupting to ask questions. As Jack proceeded, however, I became increasingly uncomfortable, for his plan differed widely from what I had envisioned and was trying to do. Having been pretty much a loner all my life, I was not an especially tactful or diplomatic person. With Jack, though, I cautiously responded so that he would not be offended by my rejection of his ideas. Much of what I had done over the years had been in labors where the responsibility was mine from beginning to end.

Essentially, Jack proposed a national body that would have total control of the leagues that evolved from it. That body would own every Little League playing field and every Little Leaguer would be a paying member.

My plan had always been almost exactly opposite. Each neighborhood league was to be autonomous. The national organization would evolve through decisions made by representatives elected by the local leagues.

Our discussion ended amicably. In retrospect, though, I can see that it was the beginning of a deep philosophical conflict. At the time, I didn't dwell on it, but sadly, such honest differences continued and grew. Six years later, they resulted in a bitter lawsuit that ended when I withdrew. I saw the financial burden it was putting on some of our top volunteers who supported my position. Thus, at the end of 1955, my national leadership of Little League came to an end.

However, busy and excited as I was about developments nationally, I somehow found time to be fully involved in helping prepare for the 11th playing season of Original Little League. Working with me throughout were the long-faithful managing personnel of the league, who, with me, made up the Little League Tournament Association: Clyde Clark, Ollie Fawcett, Howard Gair, Vance Gair, Bert Haag, John Lindemuth, Mac McCloskey, and Marty Miller. Along with planning the season's schedule of games, holding tryouts, selecting players for the teams, and conducting practice sessions, we had an even more ambitious program in mind. We intended to improve the playing field, enlarge seating capacity, complete construction of office and clubhouse, and add to our concession facilities. We saw our work as desirable not only for the local program, but also for the national tournament at the end of the season.

Williamsport was still in the process of completing the dikes and pumping stations that had been started after the great flood of 1936. The United States Corps of Engineers still had an office in the city. We had requested permission to erect part of a permanent home-run fence at the base of the earthen dike, which was their property.

Meeting with the engineer in charge and personnel from the parent office in Baltimore, I showed them our Little League movie to illustrate how important their cooperation was to us. They seemed as enthusiastic as we were about Little League's rapid growth and let us know they wanted to help as much as they could. They not only approved our immediate request, but also encouraged our long-range plan to build concrete bleachers on the entire dike area facing the playing field. As I envisioned it, that would be the last phase of increasing seating capacity.

Later that morning, Williamsport City Council echoed the engineers' approval. We also asked council to consider redesigning the West Fourth Street drainage system. During heavy rains, water from the street flowed into the third-base-dugout area and into the western end of the clubhouse. The mayor and council understood our urgent need for the clubhouse and the fact that flooding part of the field during a national or state tournament could be a major problem. We had their enthusiastic cooperation, now.

We did not overlook the boys while all of this was going on. We were pleased when a traveling salesman from Scranton, F.P. Jacobs, brought us an irresistible invitation: to bring a team of our boys to Scranton, July 24, to play one of their teams. We took a busload of boys and managing personnel and had a great time. The game, preceding a Scranton-Elmira Eastern League contest, was held on Scranton's fourth annual Boy's Day celebration, with 8,000 boys and girls in the stands. The game was a seven-inning thriller, with our team winning, 3-0.

Through the end of June and into July, I was busy at a wide variety of activities. I met with Les Lonergan and Joseph Schmidt of A.G. Spalding & Company to discuss specifications for a new Little League baseball. There were two father-son banquets, evening meetings, preparation and mailing of a questionnaire to all known functioning leagues, and a meeting with Attorney Charles F. Greevy regarding incorporation of the league. We purchased steel stands and met with our long-time supporters, the Newberry Lions Club, and the publicity committee of the Community Trade Association.

As of mid-July, we still had no sponsor for the Pennsylvania State Tournament in August. I had asked Grit Publishing Company to underwrite the cost of transportation, food, and lodging for all eight competing teams. They agreed, promising also to pick up the expense of the trophies, as they had in 1948.

At this time, I was the only paid staff. Jimmy Gehron gave me a hand when I began to tabulate the responses to the questionnaires I'd sent out in June. We prepared tournament entry forms for all the leagues we knew to be operating, and I made advance reservations for housing, meals, and entertainment. The teams making it to the finals in both the Pennsylvania and National Tournaments would never forget their Williamsport adventure if I could help it.

My days and nights were filled with meetings and other contacts. I met with several league directors and directors of nearby district tournaments. When I was not doing that, I wrote letters and made telephone calls to their counterparts in other states.

In January, the Community Trade Association, now a proponent of Little League, had proposed setting up a tournament-promotion committee. Its purpose would be to keep the National Tournament in Williamsport each year. I was in full agreement, and things got underway when they appointed a committee to work with our Tournament Association.

Before the summer was over, the CTA committee put on a drive to raise money to buy portable steel stands. The stands were to be used at the several ballfields in the city during the season and brought to Original Little League Field at tournament time. With these and the permanent stands we already had, we had seating for 3,150, not including the thousands who sat on the slope of the Lycoming Creek dike in left field.

Despite my busy schedule, I found time in early July to manage the Buick team in our league for Marty Miller. Marty was on a vacation trip with his family for the first time in the eight years I had known him. I was happy to report, when he returned, that his team had won a game, 1-0, and had played an 11-11 tie in a game called because of darkness.

Our original Little League policy was not to suspend games that had to be called, but to reschedule them as complete games. We wanted to give the boys as much opportunity to play as we could. We did not want the desire for victory to become so intense that it lessened the opportunity for them to play a full game.

That summer, I also substituted as Morning League supervisor for Bert Haag. One batter after another went to first base in my first game as Bert's substitute. The young pitcher simply couldn't locate the plate. So, from my umpiring position behind him, I called time, motioning for Mike Hoover, the center fielder, to come in. Mike had never pitched before, so I showed him how to toe the rubber and had another youngster stand at home plate as Mike took a few warmup pitches.

So that Mike would be aware of the situation, I told him there were three men on base and nobody out. He knew. But as he toed the rubber and started his pitching motion, he stopped with arms overhead. Then he lowered his arms, turned to me, face partly covered by his glove, and asked, "Shall I keep on walkin' 'em or shall I strike 'em out?" Not as the umpire, but as his manager, I said, "Strike 'em out, Mike!" We had no official scorer for Morning League games, and I don't remember who won, but I know Mike was a winner.

About midway through the season, with organizational chores done until fall, I had more freedom to do other things. By then, the office had been installed on the main floor of the new clubhouse. Jimmy Gehron and I used planks and pipe rollers to move the original 6x10-foot portable plank press box/storage room about 100 feet. It would later be used as a concession stand. We dismantled the eight-row wooden stands behind the first-base dugout and planned new, 15-tier stands along the right-field foul line. Every evening after the game, Clyde, Ollie, Howard, Vance, Johnny, Marty, Mac, and I dug a trench for the footers that would support the galvanized-steel superstructure for the new stands.

Marty, the smallest of us, drew the assignment of scaling the steel columns as we erected the superstructure. Realization of the danger Marty was in offset slightly the joy of accomplishment we felt as we worked together. Four of us at ground level would hold a column erect while two others raised a bracing member within Marty's reach from his precarious perch. Then Marty, monkey fashion, would bolt it to the column to which he was clinging. Many times, Marty repeated these tense moments over the next five years as we increased seating capacity to 5,000. The volunteers in Original Little League were a remarkable group, selfless, determined, and loyal to one another. They became lifelong friends through their common dedication to the game they helped establish for boys.

When the outfield grass died down during the unusual heat of the summer, we sought to bring it back. The small-diameter hose we used to water the skinned portion of the infield was impractical for the present purpose. My call for help to Fire Chief Michael Clark brought wonderful results. He sent 250 feet of three-inch hose and a high-capacity pump to the creek bank for us. Jimmy hooked the hose to the pump, and I started the generator.

I had barely returned to my office, as Jimmy began watering right field, when I heard excited shouting and stepped onto the press balcony to see what was going on. Park Superintendent Cliff Markle was perched atop a 30-foot ladder painting the cornice of the two-story rest-room building near the left-field foul line. He was waving his arms and hollering at Jimmy.

Jimmy, unaware of anything but what he was doing, was dragging the hose toward left field. Because of its weight and pressure, Jimmy was forced to jerk the hose along like someone cutting with a scythe. Each time he did so, the nozzle momentarily directed the water toward the ladder. When Jimmy finally realized what was happening, he stopped. No harm was done that a towel and the warm sun couldn't correct.

After a few days of watering, the grass was no longer wilted. At tournament time, the visiting press complimented us on the excellent playing facilities we had worked so hard to build.

Continuous play by Original Little League teams and by district tournament teams left the grassy area around home plate in bad condition. We had to do something to improve it before the Pennsylvania State and National Tournaments, which were nearly upon us. We called upon another community member for help, and George "Red" Hamilton, golf pro at nearby Elm Park Golf Course, came to our rescue with a sod cutter which enabled us to take up 12-inch strips of sod elsewhere for placement there.

With time running out, we enlisted the wives of managing personnel to help us do the job quickly. It was dirty work, but they got down on their hands and knees and pitched in. It *was* dirty work! We had to kneel and slide both palms under the cut squares of sod, carry them about 150 feet, and place them on the deeply raked area around the plate. We finished in the dark. The result, after we watered the newly sodded area, was a much-improved appearance of the field.

None but the faithful volunteers and their families knew how much time and effort went into the excellent facilities we provided the visiting teams at tournament time.

A WORD OF EXPLANATION

Carl E. Stotz, founder, first commissioner, and first president of Little League Baseball, Inc., died June 4, 1992. He was 82. His story of the founding and early years of the game he loved was nearing completion. It was for me, then, his friend and collaborator, to summarize from his perspective, as nearly as possible, his last six years as Little League's greatest ambassador of goodwill, its chief theoretician, and its salesman-in-chief.

Carl had authenticated all the facts in the story through Chapter 20, making the telling of the first 12 years of Little League's history indisputably his story. What follows is my attempt, without Carl's presence, to bring the story of his unrelenting crusade for little boys' baseball through 1955 to a satisfactory conclusion.

I regret that Carl is not here to put his imprimatur on the following chapters, but I know he would applaud my efforts to reflect his role in Little League in the fifties as he experienced it.

Ken Loss
September, 1992

Chapter 21

No matter how the switch of names from Little League National Tournament to Little League World Series came about, the idea was in Carl's thinking in the fall of 1947. In a letter to Charles Durban, assistant director of advertising for U.S. Rubber, seeking sponsorship of the next national tournament, Carl wrote:

"Associated Press, Newspaper Enterprise Assn. and Central Press all asked for releases during the past season and for complete coverage of our first National Tournament. With the start of the State Tournament we will keep the wires hot with releases pointing to the National. This event will be conducted with all the fanfare of a World Series, and due to its natural attraction which cannot be over-estimated, will create a tremendous public interest."

Carl, while always paying attention to detail, never felt constrained to think little. With each passing year, his vision of what Little League baseball might become grew bigger and bigger. So did the work and responsibilities for bringing it about. Hence the need for outside financing to make his full-time involvement possible.

Even with a host of dedicated volunteers, necessity demanded paid help and a division of some of the many jobs Carl had been handling almost single handed. Thus, Colonel W.H. "Cappy" Wells was brought in to direct promotion of the 1949 World Series.

The success of that series was undisputed. For the first time, teams from eight states competed for the championship. Everyone who could find a place in the bleachers or on the dike turned out for the final game. Local press and radio ecstatically reported an estimated 10,000 fans had seen New Jersey defeat Florida, 5-0. Never before had there been so large a crowd for a sporting event in Williamsport.

The biggest attraction, as always, was the boys in uniform. Another attraction was Ford Frick, president of the National League, one of the innumerable national sports figures who would appear at the Little League World Series over the years. Frick's ties to Little League became even closer when he was named a member of its first corporate board of directors. Ted Husing, popular sportscaster for NBC, also was named to the first board. Husing called the plays of the final game of the '49 World Series.

Certainly Carl's promise that the national tournament would be conducted "with all the fanfare of a World Series" had been on target. That's what happened in 1949 and continued to happen year after year thereafter.

However, it wasn't all the hoopla accompanying the games that Carl remembered with greatest joy over the years. Reminiscing near the end of his life, he said his fondest memory of Little League action was the sportsmanship of the losing team's catcher in the 1948 World Series.

The boy was 12-year-old Joe Cardamone, a good-natured kid on the Lock Haven (Pennsylvania) team. Twice in the first inning, Joe saw St. Petersburg (Florida) sluggers pound the ball over the fence. Back-to-back home runs! Each time, as they crossed the plate to score, Joe stepped up and shook his opponent's hand. He deservedly drew the admiration and cheers of the fans and ever after had a special place in Carl's heart.

Each Little League World Series sought to outdo the hospitality and excitement of the one before. The idea was to give boys and their managers, families, and fans a memorably good time while they were in Williamsport. That had been Carl's intent from the beginning of the tournaments. He worked hard, and on a grander scale, to do for the special teams that participated in the Series what he and his army of dedicated adult volunteers were doing for their leagues and teams throughout the summer. If the boys were having a healthful, well-supervised, good-spirited experience on the field, Carl maintained, they would benefit from it throughout their lives and the Little League program would continue to thrive and grow. He was Little League's most convincing preacher of the virtues of his program, and beyond doubt the most convinced. He had never questioned the purpose of Little League as he had defined it in 1940 in the Little League constitution:

(a) The object of the Little League shall be to firmly implant in the boys of the community the ideals of good sportsmanship, honesty, loyalty, courage, and reverence, so that they may be finer, stronger, and happier boys and will grow to be good, clean, healthy men.

(b) The objective will be achieved by providing supervised competitive athletic games. The supervisors shall bear in mind that the attainment of exceptional athletic skill or the winning of games is secondary, and the molding of future men is of first importance.

The special guest of the 1950 World Series from the world of professional baseball was the president of the International League, Frank Shaughnessy, who accompanied Ford Frick. To the boys, he was far more important than another honored guest, Pennsylvania's Governor James H. Duff. None in those days, however, was as big in their eyes as Carl E. Stotz, the gentle, kindly man who had made the game of baseball and the World Series, itself, a living experience for them.

The Texas victory over Connecticut, 2-1, was the first Little League World Series championship game I had seen. I was astonished at the skills the boys exhibited. I'd read about them, but seeing them was far more convincing. I, too, became a confirmed fan of organized baseball for boys.

So it went, August after August. Schoolboy Rowe, former Detroit Tiger pitching star, and Frank Leahy, legendary coach of the Notre Dame Fighting Irish football team, impressed the thousands of fans with their presence in 1951, when Connecticut turned the table on Texas, taking the series final, 3-1. These towers of national popularity, though, were not who Carl remembered best in the years that followed. His fond memory was of a boy who wasn't even on a tournament team. Darwin Cooper had won the 1951 National Soapbox Derby at Akron, Ohio, earlier in the summer. Much to Carl's delight, the Little League tournament players swarmed around Darwin, hearing his story, getting his autograph, patting him on the back. Someone who had won the Soapbox Derby was *really* important.

That year would forever be a major time in Carl's life, for on a trip across country, he became friends with his boyhood idol, major-league pitching great Cy Young. Young was 83 when they met March 7 in Canton, Ohio. They took to each other immediately.

Carl was incredulous that summer when his proposal to invite the greatest pitcher of all time to the 1951 World Series as Little League's guest wasn't unanimously approved by the board. Two members of the board, one a minor-league official himself, sought to veto Carl's suggestion. He said Cy Young was an old man who probably couldn't control his bladder, and would embarrass Little League.

Carl was incensed. Ironically, when he brought Cy Young to Williamsport anyway, the same men who'd objected to his presence were among those who surrounded him in the hotel lobby. It was obvious that they were as much in awe of the "old man" as was every other true baseball fan. Carl and the Little Leaguers couldn't even get close to him.

Carl brought his friend Cy Young to Williamsport on his own that year and every year thereafter through 1955. Cy always made a hit with the players, who plied him with questions and soaked up his many tales of diamond experiences during his long career in the majors.

That difference between Carl and some board members on that comparatively minor issue was an early warning of greater differences in the years immediately ahead. It wasn't the first, though. An earlier disagreement had occurred the year before during the Pennsylvania Tournament. When rain threatened to force play over into the following week, the same two board members had insistently proposed the final game be played on Sunday, if necessary. Carl, equally determined, flatly refused. He said he had no objection to the boys playing among themselves on Sunday if they wanted to, but Little League would not order them to play. The Pennsylvania Blue Laws were still in effect, and he was a law-abiding citizen. Little League would not, ever, order its boys to break the law, he declared. He won his point.

With a board made up primarily of national celebrities who were not hands-on Little League devotees, there began to be more and more signs that Carl's highly idealistic, single-minded leadership was being pared down. When he was advised that Howard J. Lamade, secretary of Grit Publishing Company, was to be appointed to the initial board, Carl asked that a representative of the *Williamsport Sun-Gazette* also be appointed. His request was denied. He also lost his bid to have at least half the members of the board come from the ranks of volunteer workers at the field level. He argued in vain that they would bring a better perspective of what was in the best interest of the boys than national figures, however deserving of their fame, who had no practical experience with Little League.

Carl opposed the first move to bring a "foreign" team to the World Series. The Panama Little League was made up of children of American servicemen in the Canal Zone and Panamanians who worked at the base. That, in itself, had produced controversy when the all-star team was selected. The Panamanians sought redress because, they charged, their boys had been passed up because they weren't Americans.

That wasn't what Carl wanted to hear. He needed no other reason to turn thumbs down on Panama's request to play in the World Series. But, he had another reason, a stronger reason. He wanted the August tournament to remain national, not to become international. World Series, to him, meant the National and American Leagues' best teams at the end of the season playing for the championship for that year. There were no big-league teams from outside the United States participating in that world series. He urged rejection of Panama's request.

When the board overruled him, he managed to require Panama to earn its way into the tournament by defeating a qualifying team in the United States. Panama lost its bid, making the issue moot for that year. But, the direction had been set: teams from other nations would be included in future Little League World Series. The first was Canada, in 1952. That year, by the way, Connecticut won the title for the second year in a row, eking out a 4-3 victory over Pennsylvania with a two-run sixth inning.

When Cy Young returned for the 1953 World Series, age was not his only handicap. His eyesight was failing. He could see nothing clearly beyond the infield. Now, himself an institution at the series, the record-holding 511-game winner who had pitched the first major-league no-hitter was made an honorary member of the Little League Board of Directors. That year, CBS-TV had Red Barber, the Brooklyn Dodgers' colorful play-by-play announcer, provide commentary for the film it made of the final game. The title contest was a 1-0 sqeaker of Alabama over New York.

In 1954, when New York defeated California, 7-5, for the title, no one knew that one of the unsung California players was on his way to a successful major-league career. Eight years after the series, Ken Hubbs became the Chicago Cubs' second baseman. Carl was pleased to make note of that, but he always said that producing future major-leaguers was not the primary or even a major purpose of Little League. Its purpose was to provide opportunity for fun, and help the boys develop skills and character that would serve them well for a lifetime. He believed that when properly managed according to the program he and his early associates had developed, Little League made a significant contribution to society. When he expressed such thoughts in later years, his voice would break and his eyes mist up. He felt deeply the need for such positive influence in the lives of the nation's youth.

In 1955, Pennsylvania won its second Little League World Series championship trophy. It was also Carl's last year as commissioner of Little League baseball, his last year with any ties to the organization popularly abbreviated as LLB, Inc. The Pennsylvania victory was symbolic of Carl's inner struggle as he sought victory in the game he was playing to regain control of his creation. Carl was soon to lose the struggle, and Pennsylvania, in its dramatic victory over New Jersey, had to go into overtime, winning, 4-3, in the seventh. That was the first extra-inning game in the championship round in Little League history.

While behind the scenes the drama of Carl's impending separation from the corporation was moving toward a climax — which is a story for someone more able than I to write — in the forefront at the final game of the series were Lefty Gomez, New York Yankees' pitching ace, and George M. Troutman, commissioner of minor-league baseball. Cy Young, present for the fifth successive year, was in his usual place behind third base. He had given Carl a gnarled wood cane as something tangible to remember him by when he was gone. He said Dazzy Vance, outstanding pitcher with the Detroit Tigers, had made it for him. Cy died before the next Little League season rolled around.

On the dike, behind the center-field fence, U.S. Rubber had a sign identifying itself as sponsor. In lettering so tall no fan could overlook it, the sign proclaimed: "WELCOME TO THE LITTLE LEAGUE WORLD SERIES." Before the final game, the 173rd Army Band played. Carl's promise to Jimmy and Major Gehron was continuing to be kept.

Chapter 22

Off the field, in those exciting years, the organization that oversaw Little League baseball continued to change. Carl's efforts to bring in a national sponsor had succeeded beyond anything he could have imagined in 1938 and '39. With the constant, friendly support of Charles Durban as the forties ended, Carl felt secure in his authority to maintain the program as he had guided it to that point. However, he was as uneasy about the move toward incorporation as parents are when their children begin dating or go off to college. He foresaw the possibility of his control gradually being eroded by boards of directors and corporate officials he had not appointed. To avoid that outcome, he sought Durban's assurance to the contrary within months after the corporation was established. Durban replied, March 2, 1950:

Dear Carl:

I am attaching copies of the contract proposed between yourself and Little League Baseball, Inc. On page two is the clause which I think should satisfy you on Little League coming back to you in the event of insufficient sponsorship.

Our legal counselor in talking about it says that even though there is a lot of red tape to go through to dissolve a corporation and that if somebody on the board had it in mind he could create legal obstacles, still, says Mr. Dole, "Mr. Stotz would be entitled to demand that the corporation relinquish all control over Little League Baseball in his favor regardless of completion of formal dissolution." In other words, this contract would assure you of regaining Little League regardless of whether the corporation actually dissolved or not.

That was reassuring, as far as it went, but it didn't address what might happen should Carl be superseded as president of Little League Baseball, Inc., while retaining his position as commissioner. That thought had not yet come to the surface, for with Carl as president and commissioner and his friend Charles Durban vice president and chairman of the board, they, in combination, initially wielded great influence on the board.

Besides Carl and Durban, the first corporate board included Ford C. Frick, president of the National League; Paul Kerr, vice president of the Baseball Hall of Fame; Linn C. Lightner, a Harrisburg (Pennsylvania) newspaperman; Emerson Yorke, the New York City film producer; Thomas H. Richardson, president of the Eastern League; Howard J. Lamade, Grit Publishing Company executive; Bernie O'Roarke, New England regional director of Little League; Ted Husing, prominent sportscaster; and John Lindemuth, longtime manager of an Original Little League team.

Headquarters of Little League Baseball, Inc., were set up in Williamsport with J Walter Kennedy as business manager. Kennedy had been in public relations for Notre Dame University, then for the National Basketball Association before he joined Little League. Cappy Wells was named promotion manager, operating out of New York,

Each year, new faces appeared on the board as others departed. In 1952, for example, Oliver Fawcett, manager of an Original Little league team, and J.S. Porter, West Coast field representative, joined Carl as hands-on members, replacing other hands-on members. They rarely deviated from Carl's lead. He thought at least half the board should consist of such men, but some on the board would have had to vote against themselves to bring that about.

The big change, so far as Carl was concerned, was

Peter J. McGovern's accession to the board in 1952. McGovern, a U.S. Rubber Company executive, was named to succeed Carl as president of Little League. Pete was a strong-willed businessman, with a management style far different from Carl's. In his top administrative role, he relieved Carl of much responsibility, freeing him to pursue the work he did so well, which was traveling widely all over the United States and beyond in response to requests to explain the Little League program. Carl was Little League's greatest ambassador of goodwill, its most enthusiastic advocate, its most successful salesman. Unfortunately, on many issues, he and Pete McGovern did not to see eye to eye.

For the first time, under McGovern, the presidency was a full-time job, and the president had his own office staff. Carl, as commissioner, continued to have his own secretary.

The by-laws adopted by the board for 1954-55 carefully spelled out the president's authority and responsibilities. It was the position of power in administering Little League. The revised by-laws also outlined the commissioner's duties in detail. The separation of roles greatly depleted Carl's power, making him no longer top authority, but a lesser figure than the president and chairman of the board. As Carl saw it, his power to make and enforce decisions and to name helpers unilaterally had been taken from him. He was still called on to study the program as originally intended but, in effect, only as an advisor. The change that clipped his authority, as he understood it, said:

In the fulfillment of his responsibilities and duties, the Founder and Commissioner may delegate a portion of his authority to such employees of the Corporation as may be designated with the approval of the President, but he shall retain ultimate responsibility to the Board of Directors for the proper performance thereof.

That Carl was unhappy with this development was obvious. He had conceived the idea and plan for Little League and had recruited sponsors, managers, a woman's auxiliary, and other volunteers to bring it into being. He had lovingly nurtured it during World War II. He had set its high moral tone and inspired thousands of adults to see and act on his vision. He had, almost single-handedly, sought out and persuaded U.S. Rubber to get into the act as an altruistic, not controlling, sponsor. He had worked well in that relationship, which initially maintained his control over the program. Charles Durban and he were of one mind in the idealism of a common purpose in promoting Little League.

Now, in failing health, Durban's steadying hand was less and less present. His personal assurances to Carl were not binding on officials and board members who had not been party to them. Now, more and more decisions were made that Carl thought undermined the purpose he had had in mind from the beginning, to let no goal or objective equal or superseded that of serving boys 12 and younger in his program of organized baseball. Satisfying as it was to see new leagues and thousands more boys come into the program annually, that should not be a primary goal of Little League, Carl insisted. He felt some who now had more clout in policy-making than he neither understood nor respected his position. He was convinced most volunteers in the field did.

To a majority of board members, Carl's complaints

founder-commissioner and the corporation's chief executive. As it turned out, their differences proved irreconcilable, and Carl withdrew to private life. Neither party was graceful in the divorce, their differences being too great for caring third parties to effect a reconciliation. By then, there were more than 3,000 Little Leagues.

No one currently involved in directing the international baseball program for boys and girls was a party to that 1950's dispute. Presumably, none has reason to feel guilty about what happened. Let it suffice that the program continues, and the example of thousands of conscientious adult volunteers is helping guide the minds and hearts of innumerable youngsters toward a better tomorrow.

Chapter 23

World Series and the differences in leadership goals and procedures were not the whole story of Carl's six years with Little League Baseball, Inc. His wide travels, always in response to requests from people he visited, were adventures in themselves.

In mid-December, 1949, a couple of weeks before incorporation was completed and the initial corporate officers and board of directors were announced, Carl and Grayce were in Havana, Cuba, where Carl was talking up Little League.

Carl's most poignant memory of that trip was of boys in Havana playing ball with make-do equipment. They used broomsticks for bats and tightly wound strips of worn-out inner tubes for balls. If any kids needed sponsored leagues, they did, and some were formed soon afterward.

The following month saw Carl in Texas. On his way back, he made a joint appearance in Joplin, Missouri, with Baseball Commissioner A.B. "Happy" Chandler. In spreading the gospel of Little League from state to state and in foreign lands, Carl was happy. He appreciated the respect with which he was received wherever he went and the many courtesies accorded him. He was steadily on the move doing what he did best, selling the Little League program to a host of receptive customers. One year, he spoke to 249 groups who had requested his visits.

Occasionally, Carl took his family with him, but wherever they went, Carl spoke at scheduled Little League meetings. While they were in California, Carl was finally able to introduce his family to Sam Porter, the man he depended on most to help the Little League movement

spread on the West Coast. Sam was an enthusiastic sup-
porter of Little League who, like many other field representatives, became Carl's life-long friend and admirer.

No doubt about it, though, the highlight of the trip
for the Stotz girls was not Little League promotion, but a
tour of the MGM Studios, where they saw several movies
in production, including one starring screen-idol Robert
Taylor.

The Stotzes returned by way of a northern route so
Carl could continue to tell the Little League story in more
communities across the country.

It seemed unlikely that any trip would ever top the
1951 cross-country trip. Their crystal ball hadn't shown
them what awaited them two years later in Canada. To this
day, their vacation in Canada the summer of 1953 tops all
experiences the girls had with their parents while Carl was
the best-known figure in Little League. They drove to
Boston and boarded a ferry to Yarmouth, Nova Scotia. Carl
spoke in Halifax, Glace Bay, Sydney, and nearby communities. The Canadians sang their national anthem before each
meeting. That impressed Carl. Everywhere they went,
their hosts treated them like royalty. The Canadians held
banquets and put on parades in Carl's honor as founder of
Little League.

Carl's most far-reaching trip for Little League came
in 1955, his last year with the organization. At the request
of the United States Department of Defense, he and John
Lindemuth, executive secretary of Little League, visited
American military bases in Germany, England, France, Italy,
and Morocco. They were flown in a military plane out of
Andrews Air Force Base.

The Little League emissaries were expected to
interest service personnel with families abroad to form

leagues for their sons. Ever the optimist about the ability of properly supervised sports to break down racial, cultural, ethnic, economic, social, and language barriers, Carl regretted not being permitted to reach out to all the boys in the countries he visited. He believed introducing American baseball through the children would help heal the scars of World War II. At the time, that view was not popular with military officials.

Carl and John began their month-long itinerary in Europe and Africa May 5, touching down first in Germany. Their first visit with Americans abroad was at Garmisch-Partenkirchen, a Bavarian resort center near the Austrian border used by the military. They were treated as honored guests by General Anthony C. McAuliffe, commanding general of the 7th Army in Germany, the man who headed the Berlin airlift in 1948 and '49. He is the general who said "Nuts!" to the Germans when they demanded his surrender at Bastogne during the war. His wife arranged a tea in the guests' honor. That was as close to royal treatment as they could get from the Americans!

Again, Carl made a sale, and Little League gained a foothold among servicemen's children in Europe. After flights to England, France, and Italy, and numerous meetings in each, the Stotz-Lindemuth mission moved on. On the way to North Africa, their plane put down briefly at the sea-level airport by the Rock of Gibralter. Carl, the tourist, soon found himself on the receiving end of a curt order when he walked onto the runway to get a better camera angle of the Rock.

"Get off the runway!" a commanding voice barked over the loudspeaker. "Planes are coming in!"

Carl obeyed.

The travelers found Casablanca, Morocco, a place

of stark contrasts. In one section of the city, the stench was so pervasive they held their noses as they walked down the streets past the many open shops. Their hotel, on the other hand, was in an elegant part of the city. To find respite from the squalid inner city, Carl went for a solitary walk on the beach. Wanting to sit there and enjoy the sea, he decided to rent a chair from a concessionaire. But, Carl neither spoke nor understood his language. Using hand signs, he finally made his want known. He probably paid much more for the chair than the locals would have, but he had his view and sat back and relaxed.

However awestruck, the tourists did not forget their mission: to introduce the boys of the American military to Little League so they, too, could say they had been Little Leaguers when they returned to America. They met with interested adults in the base theater, which Carl described as being "like an immense tent." After they had said their piece and answered many questions, they took in a movie with the G.I.s. They had many meetings like that on their trip.

Carl was ever watchful for positive ways to bring Little League to the attention of more people. He had had a big hand in reaching *Reader's Digest*, which ran Mrs. Baldwin's article on the program in 1951. Carl seized every chance to channel information and anecdotes about Little League to inquiring journalists. No publication was too large or too small to elicit his helpful response.

Though constantly on the run, Carl somehow managed to collaborate with Mrs. Baldwin in writing the book *At Bat With Little League* in 1951-52. They said their narrative-style documentary had taken a year to produce, and they assured their readers that everything they'd written was true, except the names.

Newsreels were still a regular feature at movie theaters, and brief segments of Little League World Series play showed up on them. Interest in Little League spread rapidly as the news media told and retold the story. From one league in 1939, the program had grown to 17 in 1947, when the first national tournament was held. By 1952, with ever-increasing media attention, it had become more than 88 times bigger, with a total of 1,500 known leagues. That year, Carl lived contentedly in Paradise. He wrote:

> *As a boy I could never have enough baseball, but now I am having the thrill of my life. Every Little League game is always a new thrill. Every time I hear the umpire say, "Play ball!" it's a payoff for me.*

Carl's last big opportunity for telling his and the Little League story directly to a national audience while he was commissioner came in 1955. Ralph Edwards, genial host of This Is Your Life, had asked him to be a subject. Family, friends, key associates, and so on would be brought to New York at the show's expense. What a great opportunity, Carl thought — until he learned one of the show's sponsors was a cigarette company. For him to appear under those auspices, Carl said, would send the wrong signal to the boys, whom he always encouraged to avoid using tobacco products and alcohol. His decision not to appear on the show cost the founder of Little League $1,000, the fee he had been offered. He had no regrets.

Chapter 24

Carl Stotz and other Little League Baseball officials cooperated with Hy Turkin, who assembled and edited *The Official Encyclopedia of Little League Baseball*, published in 1954 by Little League Baseball, Inc. If some of the following tales Carl told me sound familiar, you probably read Turkin's version in Chapter 10 of that volume.

"Most of us who have become deeply involved in Little League over the years," Carl said, "are unknown outside their own communities. On occasion, though, some nationally known baseball figure finds the small-boy version of the game irresistible. One such was Jack Norworth, writer of the baseball classic *Take Me Out to the Ball Game*.

"When he penned the song in 1906, Norworth, himself, was not a fan. Baseball enthusiasts had been singing his tune for decades before he got around to seeing his first game — in 1942. That game hooked him for the rest of his life.

"In 1950, by then an avid fan, Jack founded the Laguna Beach (California) Little League and served as its commissioner. It was one of the first on the West Coast."

After Carl left Little League Baseball, Inc., journalists, radio and TV talk-show hosts, and others who dote on controversy annually contacted him to stir up old issues. Fair enough. He responded as best he could, but always, he preferred to talk about the positive things he had promoted, the heartwarming success stories with Little League ties that kept coming to his attention. He found pleasure in occassionally rereading a paragraph in a letter by Richard A. Snyder, a field representative, to Pete McGovern in 1955:

> Sometime after our early beginning [of the league Snyder helped to build], I had the good fortune to meet Carl Stotz and immediatlely marveled at his ability to understand all the problems of boys and adults as related to the program. The only way to describe my admiration for him is to say that, if God had been asked to create a man who would have all the knowledge, patience, and understanding to lead a boys' program, He would have created Carl Stotz.

The adulatory attitude of that one field representative toward Carl was not uncommon. Carl's highly successful salesmanship was no carefully plotted technique. He sincerely believed and tried to practice what he preached. His was a down-to-earth message. His listeners bought into the program because they believed in the messenger.

In a 1980 letter addressed to "Carl Stotz, FOUNDER, Little League Baseball," Stephen Brockway of Council Bluffs, Iowa, thanked Carl for his healthful influence when he, Brockway, was a Little Leaguer in Williamsport in the early fifties. He said he was now the father of five and a teacher who had been honored in three different schools as Teacher of the Year. He wrote that Carl had taught him how to win gracefully and how to lose with dignity.

"I respect you for that," Brockway wrote.

'I remember, after one particular game that we lost (what a squeaker!), that you put your arm around me and said, 'I'm so proud of you. I think you pitched your best game, ever!'

" 'But, we lost!' I answered back.

'And you smiled at me again, 'But think what you

have won! Can anyone ever ask you to do better than your best?'

"Your personal encouragement, fortified by the most important institution of my youth, taught me more about manhood than any other game I would play, more about the values giving of self for others than any other teacher I would have.

'I love you for that....'

"As for the kids, if only I could count the times I've told young spirits, 'No one can ask you to do better than your best!'"

Carl was always alert for examples of adults who showed special interest in supporting Little League baseball, like P.K. Wrigley, owner of the Chicago Cubs, who assisted 56 leagues, some with $1,000 grants, in 1953. Or Eddie Dyer, manager of the St. Louis Cardinals, who sponsored an early Little League team in Houston, Texas. Once when the Cardinals had a day off, Dyer flew home just to see his Little Leaguers in action.

"One of the Little League's boosters in the late forties and early fifties who impressed me most," Carl said, "was Mrs. Christine Gehrig, mother of the great New York Yankee first baseman. Mrs. Gehrig served on the first board of directors of the Milford (Connecticut) Little League. When the league named its park in honor of her son, she helped dedicate the Lou Gehrig Memorial Field. She continued her work for the Milford League until she died, early in 1954."

Only once in major-league baseball has there been a double no-hitter. The year was 1917, between the Chicago Cubs and the Cincinnati Reds. "The first time it happened in Little League Baseball, so far as I am aware," Carl said, "was in 1950. In Bellefonte, Pennsylvania, Ron

Brooks and Billy Sharp each held the opposition hitless until darkness forced a halt and the game had to be replayed later."

Carl was pleased when Little League Baseball, Inc., recently came up with leagues for children with physical handicaps. He favored making the game available to as many children as want to play. He was well aware that some handicapped boys had managed to play on regular teams, but they were the exceptions. Bobby McDowell is an example.

"Bobby was handicapped," Carl said. "He had no left leg from just below the knee since he was two years old. That didn't prevent him from taking the mound for Windber, Pennsylvania, in the opening game of the season in 1950 to overpower the opposing batters, striking out 13. Meanwhile, he went two for three at the plate, driving in the run that gave his team a 3-2 victory. The only concession made in his behalf was a courtesy runner.

"Two years later, a gritty, determined, 11-year-old showed the people of Sherman Oaks, California, how to rise above 'insurmountable' handicaps. Nelson Gary, Jr., had no right arm; it had been amputated when he was three. At that time, Pete Gray, a one-armed professional, played regularly for the Southern Association's Memphis Chicks. Gray's inspiring performance drew national attention and led Nelson's dad to take his 3-½-year-old son to Memphis to visit him. The result was good advice from Gray on how to exercise the armless shoulder. He kept up a long-time correspondence with Nelson. Gray went on to a brief career with the St. Louis Browns in the American League. Nelson and his dad had chosen a worthy role model. Nelson became a capable Little Leaguer despite his handicap.

192 | A Promise Kept

"In 1953, in New Jersey, another determined youngster excelled despite physical limitations. Although he walked with a limp as a result of polio when he was five, Tommy O'Donnell ignored his handicap once the game started. The astonishing result was that he became both a pitching and hitting star in the Keansburg Little League. Two of his games were no-hitters. He also led the league in batting. Tommy proved physical handicaps are no match for a positive attitude and natural ability."

Carl's point with such stories was that the people who organized and directed Little Leagues were caring people. Most leagues had no players with major physical handicaps, but all who exemplified the prevailing spirit of Little League were eager to give every interested and capable lad a chance. It was this spirit, not the creation of a flood of future professional stars, that made Little League baseball so dear to him.

Never conclude that because a certain pattern of performance holds most of the time, it will always be so, Carl liked to point out. He said 12-year-olds were generally the best pitchers and hitters in Little League because they were bigger, better coordinated, and more experienced. Sometimes though, a younger, smaller boy excels early. He like to cite the case of eight-year-old Gene Burke, Jr.

"In 1953," he said, "Gene, a sturdy 4-foot-10 92-pounder, was a competent catcher and a better-than-average switch-hitter in the Hicksville (Long Island) Little League. Gene's claim to Little League fame came not from his catching or hitting, but from his pitching. He was called on unexpectedly when his team was temporarily short-handed in that position. In successive starts six days apart, Gene threw back-to-back no-hitters, striking out 16 in one game and 14 in the other."

Carl smiled at the thought of how disconcerted the older and bigger boys on the team must have felt. Gene had taught them a good lesson in humility.

Someone else who had been momentarily disconcerted in the early fifties, Carl said, was his good friend Sam Porter. Sam had become so consumed with the desire to help spread Little League opportunities throughout the West Coast that it seemed he was always going anywhere but home. At least, that's the way it seemed to Sam's wife.

"One night when he came home very late," Carl told me, chuckling at the story he was about to tell, "Sam quietly got ready for bed and tiptoed into the bedroom without turning on the light. He didn't want to disturb his wife.

"As he was about to turn back the cover and ease himself into bed, he noticed the dim outline of a figure beside his wife. His heart sank. What had he done, rarely being home anymore during normal waking hours?

"Then Sam ripped back the cover to be greeted by a bizarre sight and the gleeful laughter of his very-much-awake wife. He laughed with her as he removed the catcher's mask for its head position, the chest protector with a rolled up blanket beneath it, the shin guards, and the shoes and joined his wife in bed."

"When talking about the impossible schedule Sam was keeping and remonstrating with him had shown no results, Mrs. Porter decided to turn his interest in everything Little League to her advantage. In telling me about it, Sam said it had worked!"

Carl was proud, too, of the wonderful results that came about when leagues conscientiously abided by his undeviating insistence that players should never be selected for leagues or teams for any reason but ability to perform.

"We always assumed," he said, "that if a youngster was capable of playing and his parents were willing, he could be a member of a team. Our first Little League national champions were an all-American team. The Maynard Midgets in Williamsport were a mixture of races, religious backgrounds, and ethnic origins. The boys were representative of the area within the league's boundaries. The mix differs from league to league, depending on the makeup of the neighborhood. Little League has never been pro or anti any segment of American society, and I pray it never will be."

One of the finest examples of how the all-American approach worked at best, as Carl told it, occurred in New York City when the Protestant Council organized a Little League in the lower east side of Manhattan. By Little League rules, every boy under 13 within the league boundaries was eligible to try out. In this case, the local Catholic church urged its youngsters to participate. B'nai B'rith, a Jewish service organization, provided the uniforms. Interfaith and interracial cooperation was easy when no one made an issue of it. The result was a program as integrated as the abilities of the boys permitted. Every race was involved. The goal wasn't integration; that was the welcome by-product in this and other leagues when only ability was considered when choosing players.

As Carl was about to part from Little League Baseball, Inc., and never return, Albert E. Houghton, the corporation's secretary-treasurer, said of him, "I always considered the name of Stotz and Little League to be synonymous." So, too, had all but a handful of the millions who knew about the program at that time, so think the millions who have been privileged to know of Carl's dedicated labors to translate an ideal into a commonplace experience for youngsters not only in America, but in many lands around the world.

Someone who has done so well by so many over so long a period of time deserves more compelling words than I can write. In Carl's correspondence, I found those words in a letter from the mother of a player on the Morrisville (Pennsylvania) team that played in the 1955 Little League World Series. She wrote:

Dear Mr. Stotz:

Even though I have never met you, I like you very much. I am Tony Cigarran's mother. (He was) shortstop for Morrisville, and I am writing at a moment when my heart is filled with gratitude.

These past weeks I have followed the Little League games closely. I saw the boys who couldn't hold back the tears when they lost, and the ones who shouted with relief when they won. I saw the mothers who quietly swallowed an aspirin in tense moments, and the fathers who used paper cups to make themselves heard. I saw the boys who unconsciously blessed themselves at bat and the ones who silently prayed to "'let it be this time." I watched the boys as they proudly signed books and articles and collected names and addresses. I saw all this and wondered at the wonderful thing you started.

My husband's work is taking us out of the States. We should have gone two weeks ago, but putting first things first changed our plans so Tony could play ball. My first concern on leaving was the fear that he would forget the greatness of his country. I never wanted him to lose the feeling of America. I bought books on the lives of great Americans, a large map of the United States, and a bronze plaque of Abraham Lincoln to try to impress him quickly, but after the experience of these past weeks, I am not afraid.

No one can ever make him forget Ernie the policeman who took him to Mass or John the bus driver who cheered him on, or his adopted Uncles who paid the forty-dollar bill for hamburgers, and the many happy moments with his teammates and coaches, but most important, I am sure, he will never forget our National Anthem, so now I am relaxed and happy. I just wish I could shake your hand and say, "Thank you, Mr. Stotz, for giving my son America."

Sincerely,
Dara Cigarran

LEFT FIELD FOUL LINE - 171'

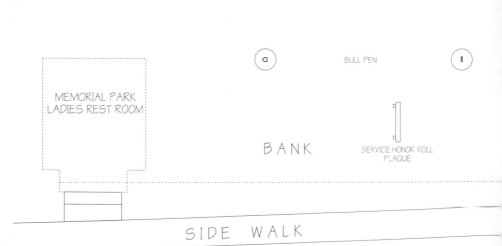

BULL PEN

⊲

ı

MEMORIAL PARK
LADIES REST ROOM

BANK

SERVICE HONOR ROLL
PLAQUE

SIDE WALK

CURB

WEST FOURTH STREET
HIGHWAY ROUTE 220